RESEARCH
In Church
and Mission

Viggo Søgaard

William Carey Library

Pasadena, California

Published by
William Carey Library
P. O. Box 40129
Pasadena, California 91114
(818) 798-0819

Library of Congress Cataloging-in-Publication Data

Søgaard, Viggo
    Research in church and mission / Viggo Søgaard
        p.   cm.
    Includes bibliographical references.
    ISBN 0-87808-271-9   (alk. paper)
    1.   Communication--Religious aspects--Christianity--Study and
teaching.   2. Mission of the church.   3. Missions--Theory.
4. Missions--Study and teaching.   I. Title.
BV4319.S647   1996
266' . 007'2--dc21   96-48337
                                                                          CIP

Printed in the United States of America

CONTENTS

i

SECTION II
SURVEY RESEARCH

SECTION III
SPECIAL APPLICATIONS OF RESEARCH

LIST OF FIGURES

ACKNOWLEDGMENTS

In presenting a book on research, I am much aware of the fact that much of the content is something I have learned from others. Some material is original, some is gained through personal experience in research, but much is learned from teachers, authors, colleagues, and students. A list of acknowledgments will therefore never be complete. Nevertheless, there are some who deserve special thanks and must be mentioned.

First of all, I want to express my gratitude to Dr. James F. Engel who taught me much about research, and I would in particular express my thanks for his kindness in letting me use sections of the material in his book *How Can I Get Them To Listen.*

Thanks to Dr. Bryant Myers of MARC for writing the foreword. My interactions with him in various research projects have been a challenge and a joy.

My thanks also go to my son, Kim, who has designed the cover of this book. He has shown his creative talents by integrating both a research symbol as well as the cross to signify both the content and purpose of the book.

Thanks to the many students I have had the privilege to teach research at Fuller Seminary School of World Mission. As we together have struggled with research issues in church and mission, much of the content of this book has been refined, extended, and made more useful.

To the many friends and fellow servants of our Lord who have in some way contributed to this book, I give my sincere thanks. I have attempted to acknowledge sources in the text or in footnotes. To those who should have been acknowledged in the text or in footnotes, but have been omitted due to error or lack of information on my part, I give my apologies.

I am also grateful to Else Marie Larsen and Anne E. White for their help with getting the text and material into a good format.

My primary purpose for writing this book has been to provide a tool that will assist Christian workers to be effective communicators. It is dedicated to the many who in one way or another have had a part in the making of the text.

Viggo Søgaard

FOREWORD

RESEARCH? WHAT FOR?

Research and Christian mission sadly do not often go together as well as they might. Mission leaders, strategists and practitioners tend to see research as something that serves to occupy space on library shelves or make piles for dust collection in the office of academics. Researchers tend to see leaders and practitioners as people making decisions and spending money without the facts, leading by whim and intuition.

This is of course an overstatement. Christians in mission have often done considerable study before they enter a new location or people group. Large reports, measured in kilograms, are often produced. This kind of research is expected and done. Contextualization is accepted dogma now. Studying the local culture and language is important so that we can answer the question: How can we best package or present the gospel in this place or to this people? Planning and strategy formulation are also the norm in Christian mission today. We've all been converted to the importance of effective management and good planning. Somewhere in the institution, there is a planning researcher spewing out studies and reports. Strategic planning documents now rival country and people research for pages of paper consumed.

Søgaard encourages us to go beyond this dichotomy between research and the real world of our practice. He proposes that research is where the real learning and help comes from. Testing our strategy against our experience, and listening to those we seek to serve, is where the real value of research lies. The research that is not so often done by Christians is the kind that allows our audiences to speak for themselves, the kind of research that asks such questions as: What message have people heard? What impact do they say our work has had?

Why is this important?

LEARNING OUR WAY INTO THE FUTURE

We used to believe that the world and how it worked could be understood, at least in its essential elements. This meant that smart people could create clever strategies and plans that would change the world. "Management by objectives" said it all. The world, properly researched, could be understood and hence managed through effective planning. Objectives could be set and then met by following a blueprint or plan of action.

This view of the world is increasing problematic. The grand plans and elegant strategies haven't worked so well. Good things happened, bad things happened, but little went according to plan. We now know that social systems are counter-intuitive. A social system can be mapped, but there are so many feedback loops that linear logic has no predictive power. Every time the best and the brightest plan another social program intended to ameliorate a particular social problem, the only thing we can count on are unintended consequences.

Does this mean that we throw planning out the window? Is the answer to non-linear social systems and their unpredictability simply to work in a random or *ad hoc* manner? No, of course not. It does mean, however, that our points of emphasis in the planning process must change.

The need for a vision, that direction into the future toward which we believe we are called to move, is inarguable. A vision and the values that explain how we will move toward the vision are essential for us and for those we lead. We still need planning, but planning of a different kind.

Planning in an unpredictable environment must become more short-term. If the world around us is changing rapidly, then we must lift our heads and look to the horizon more frequently. We must check our position and trajectory in comparison to our vision more often, lest our turbulent environment push us radically off course unawares and we invest our work in directions we do not wish to go.

Once we know where we are and what our trajectory is we can reorient ourselves so that we are pointing toward our vision once again. Then we re-plan and work for a while before we stop again and check our bearings. And so it goes: we plan, evaluate, plan, evaluate and plan again. Our vision keeps us oriented, but it is our research and evaluation that become the critical success factor. The emphasis has moved from the planning, which is now always contingent and tentative, to the research which tells us where we actually are at any point in time. We no longer plan our way into the future as much as we learn our way.

THE THREE PILLARS OF RESEARCH THAT HELP US LEARN OUR WAY INTO THE FUTURE

Søgaard's point of departure in this book is significant. We must always understand research in terms of our wish to become more effective in our communications. After all, Christian mission is knowledge work, managing information so that it can be accepted and used. Thus, communication is what mission is most fundamentally about. Effective communication is what good mission strategy is for. The vision is for a world that has heard and responded. God is a communicator and we are to be communicating with God and with each other about God.

Søgaard imbeds his explanation of the why and how of research in a model of communication that assumes that both the message sender and the message hearer have something important to say that the other needs to hear. The purpose of research is to help each understand the other so that communication about the meaning is effective. This is how learning takes place. Learning is about relationships and dialogue—hearing one another.

Søgaard's approach to research then takes another important step. Research must be driven by what we need to know. This is a break with the other dominant model of research often taught in Christian mission, the one that says that you should go out and collect all the information you can find and then try to figure out what it means. Søgaard's needs-based approach starts with the mission executive or mission strategist asking the question, "What do I need to know?" and then using research to go and find the information necessary to answer the question. What we need to know is where we are in terms of how the people we serve are changing and experiencing our ministry. What we need to know is how the rapidly changing context in which we work has diverted or redirected our plans so that we no longer are properly oriented to our vision.

Søgaard's research framework also contains another important distinctive. If the purpose of research is to help us learn our way into the future, then Søgaard rightly demands that research be driven by those who manage or carry out the communication process, not by researchers themselves. There is no research for the sake of research here. Mission executives and those who design and carry out mission strategy are the ones responsible for setting the vision and making sure their work is pointing toward that vision. Thus, they are the ones whom research serves and hence must be the ones who provide leadership to the research process. Søgaard's framework for relating management and the researcher (Figure 1.4) is very important. Søgaard understands that research directed by and answering the questions of management or the mission strategist is the key to research making a difference.

WHAT SHOULD WE DO?

This book is written first for the mission leader, the strategist and the practitioner. Those of us in this camp need to understand what research is really for and what makes research useful, affordable and helpful. We need to understand enough about the why and how of research so that we can carry out our responsibility to guide research and evaluation work and then properly apply what is learned. Søgaard's *Research in Church and Mission* helps us do this.

This book is also written for those who work in places where professional research people are hard to come by. It is also a how-to book for those who want to begin the journey toward professionalism in the doing of research. *Research in Church and Mission* is insightful, practical and full of examples. Those of us who aspire to do research would do well to begin the journey here.

Dr. Bryant L. Myers
Director of Missions Advanced Research and Communication Center
Monrovia, California
2 October 1996

INTRODUCTION

Back in 1969, a colleague of mine found out about a research project being done in East Thailand. It was a study in which they were trying to understand people's attitudes to certain words and concepts. My colleague then asked the researchers to include two more words in the study: Christ and Christian.

The response format used in this study was a +/-3 scale. Interestingly, the response to the word Christ was a positive 3. Jesus as a person intrigues people, and I have never seen a negative response to Jesus in a research study. The Buddhist see him as a key religious figure, and the Muslim place him next to Mohammed. It would probably be difficult to find an atheist that would give a negative response to the person Jesus.

On the other hand, the word Christian received a negative 2 in this particular study, and many readers will probably recognize the situation and feel empathy. This is not the end of the story, as we shall see later, but the results were of extreme importance to the ministry I was personally involved in at that time. At the Voice of Peace Studios in Chiangmai, we were producing Christian radio programs for this audience. We immediately realized that we had to be extremely careful as to how we used words in our radio programs. Asking people to be Christians was—at that time—something to be avoided, but, on the other hand, we could ask them to be followers of Jesus. We also realized that careful teaching about Jesus was needed.

As we took a closer look at the situation, we realized that the reason for the negative response was ready at hand. The year was 1969, and we were at the height of the Vietnam war. The research was done in an area close to an American air base. Further study revealed that in the minds of the people, a Christian was a white person, and the "white people" they saw were soldiers who were in the middle of a war, and who sought relaxation and relief from the war in the bars that cluttered the streets around the base.

It was important to realize that something needed to be done. Fortunately, Thai Christian students were getting active in evangelism, providing a "Thai face" to the word *Christian*. Mass media was also used extensively to teach the gospel, and there was an increasing use of Thai music and Thai Christian testimonies in media programs.

A significant change was seen over the next few years. In a study among students in Thailand, from grade 5 through college, conducted in 1974, we found that among the student population of Thailand, the word Christian had become a neutral word. Five years later, a large study was conducted among 21 sub-groups in the city of Bangkok, and the word Christian was then understood as a positive. On the scale referred to above, it was between one and two on the positive side. We could then readily ask people to become Christians. Due to the differences in the study populations we cannot compare these results directly, but there seemed to be a real shift.

The illustration is given here to underline the importance of good information, and good information is usually obtained through some kind of planned research. If we look at the Bible, we are told that Jesus knew what people were thinking or what was in their minds. We will not try to compare ourselves to him, but we can compare our approach to his. By having good information we will know what people are thinking in response to our messages.

Engaging in research is primarily a question of attitudes. A "research mind" is someone who will do whatever is necessary to gain as much information as possible about the audience in order to communicate the love of God effectively to them. We also call this receptor-oriented communication, and, according to Charles Kraft, in receptor-orientation the sender—you or me—will pay whatever the cost is to achieve communication with the other person.

Unfortunately, research has not always been readily acceptable to Christian leaders. We have seen the term itself being rejected due to theological reasons such as, "only God can truly evaluate the effectiveness of our ministry." With this we do not disagree, but it is our contention that research must be seen as a valuable and indispensable dimension of effective and accountable ministries. If we want to be good stewards of God-given resources there is no reason to be scared of research or having our ministries evaluated.

Actually, research is a non-threatening daily phenomenon that we all engage in, one way or another, as we seek information from or about each other, and the surrounding environment. A look out the window to see if it is raining could be called research, and a study of the religious convictions of our audience is also research. In our desire to be accountable and good stewards, we should have no theological problems viewing research as a legitimate and indispensable tool of communication. We all want to know if people understand our message, or if anyone is listening to our radio programs.

The rationale and purpose for using research in church and mission can be summed up in a few preliminary questions:

1. *What do I need to know?*
2. *Why do I need to know this?*
3. *Where can I get the information?*
4. *From whom do I need the information?*
5. *When do I need it?*
6. *How will I use the information?*
7. *What will be the result of using this information?*

The purpose of this book is, then, to provide the reader with the insights and skills needed to utilize reliable research methodologies that in turn will provide valuable information on how to conduct our ministry in the most effective way. In section one, an introduction to the topic will be given, and then chapters 2 and 3 will give a communication and strategy context to research. Section two, covering chapters 4 to 12 will take us through the various stages of a survey research project, from design, through sampling, questionnaire construction, field work, and tabulation and reporting. Section three will provide a few chapters on special research topics. Chapter 13 will treat media research in particular, and chapter 14 will give an example of a research project where new approaches were developed. Finally, chapter 15 will provide a glossary of important research terms.

Section I

RESEARCH IN PERSPECTIVE OF COMMUNICATION

1

A RESEARCH AND INFORMATION SYSTEM

How do we get information that will make us relevant and effective in our church and missionary tasks? How do we achieve intelligent and effective use of media? How do we measure the results of our work? It is such questions this book will seek to answer by introducing research methodologies and techniques that are available to us and how they can function in the service of Christian ministry and communication. The book will also provide basic teaching that will help us develop research skills.

INFORMATION THAT MAKES US RELEVANT

For our ministry, we need reliable and valid information. Broadcasters may be tempted to just count letters from listeners to judge effectiveness, or the evangelist may be satisfied with counting decisions to prove that observed changes were caused by our particular ministry or program. By approaching research from such a perspective we will be focusing on single issues or causes. We need to support such claims by reliable research. In reality, results will often be caused by a combination of activities, so if we only focus on one or two observable factors, our attention may be diverted from the real causes. The public crusade meeting may be able to count the decisions, but the primary cause or reason for a response may be the constant, faithful witness by local churches in a community.

Likewise, we need a common frame of reference when comparing results. One person may say that they can win more people in one week by personal evangelism than a radio station can do in a whole year. On the other hand, the broadcaster talks about the millions being reached. Both may be partly right, but they are wrong in their assumptions. An important question that would need to be asked is, how and for what purpose is each medium or approach being used.

The effects of communication can also be hindered by a variety of causes. For example, in a Muslim context an unfortunate choice of message may create barriers. Topics such as eating pork, freedom of women, music, or Christian names are all problematic and may cause resistance or even hostility in such contexts. We may wrongly interpret this as resistance to the gospel, so we need to be extremely careful when we try to explain or interpret so-called non-responsiveness.

WHO SHOULD DO THE RESEARCH?

It may be more important to start by asking, *Who needs the information?* This topic will be treated in more detail later, but as research requires a certain attitude more than a set of skills, we can say that information is primarily needed for decision-making. It is for the leaders who desire to have accurate information on which they can base their planning and evaluate the ministry.

To respond to the question in the heading, *Who should do the research?* the answer would be, *It all depends on what kind of research.* Research is a technical task, requiring certain skills, but both management and producers need to be involved in the process if you are to safeguard relevant data collection and actual use of the information. The management need, first of all, to be involved in planning the research and the establishment of research objectives, and then later be involved in the interpretation and application of the data. The actual data collection in a survey research project, involving questionnaires, is the task of a researcher.

But, there are many kinds of research we all can take part in. Any producer can spend time with representatives of the audience, asking questions and getting to know them. One radio speaker told me that whenever he got on a bus, he would try to find a seat next to someone who looked like his "target" audience. He then used the opportunity to talk with the person to discover their interests and concerns. Another person told me that whenever he got into a taxi and the driver resembled the people he was ministering to, he would immediately try to start a conversation to discover what was important to that person.

We all need a research perspective, a research attitude, so that we at all times are seeking good and important information. As a ministering team, we also need a common concern for research so that information gathering can be a joint effort. If it is just left to the researcher, the result may be research reports sitting on shelves without being used.

My personal perspective is primarily a marketing research perspective, but strongly influenced by intercultural experiences. A marketing-based research concept implies a deeply involved role for research in the management decision-making process. Such a perspective suggests that we only gather the information we need according to stated objectives. This may, for example, be the development of a strategy or the selection of relevant biblical texts for a program or printed booklet. The key will therefore be to know what we need to know.

If we are to be effective as Christian communicators we need a good information system that will provide us with reliable data. In the following two chapters we shall look at the function of research in Christian communication and the development of strategy for our churches, organizations and missions. The framework is the field of communication, but communication is understood in a broad sense. It involves more or less all aspects of Christian ministry.

A RESEARCH AND INFORMATION SYSTEM

An organization with a good research and information system will view research as an ongoing function and not just as a task of gathering data and analyzing the data for useful information. A research system implies that research functions as an integral part of the decision-making process by management and leadership. As such, researchers are viewed as involved and responsible participants in this process. Their task is one of providing meaningful and useful information that will reduce error, result in better decisions, and in the end ensure a higher level of stewardship.

In such an integrated system, research will help the organization to focus its resources on the real task and the intended audience. It is, therefore, an audience-oriented approach to ministry and communication activities. Fortunately, more and more churches, missions, and Christian organizations are accepting such a perspective in which research is seen as an indispensable function.

The question will often be asked, how much money do we need to spend on research? This question will be treated later in this book, but one helpful way to decide on the extent of a research and information system is, first of all, to identify potential barriers to our work as well as bridges that can help us reach our goals. These are the critical success factors of the church or mission involved.

The term Critical Success Factors is borrowed from an article on systems evaluation in *Newsweek* in 1984 by Gerrity and Crescenzi. In the article, "Designing Information Systems that Work," they described how an organization can build a cost-efficient information system based on the company's actual needs for information, which in turn is based on critical success factors. Effectiveness does not, according to the authors, begin by designing an elaborate data-processing system, but by identifying the company's critical success factors, that is, the things managers do that are crucial to achieving their business objectives.

It is my experience that the process of identifying the critical success factors often proves to be as important as the actual end results. Interestingly, even a secular company producing a simple product will often find that four out of five top critical success factors will be in the area of human relations. The manufacturing of quality products is obviously critical, but so is the relationship between managers, the working climate for the staff, the relationship to clients, and other areas of relationships.

Applying the process of identifying critical success factors to the planning of Christian mission has been attempted by this author a number of times and has proved to be a most helpful activity. The process has proved to be a powerful tool in the planning process. If critical success factors are identified and put in order of priority, the management will be able to concentrate on the most important factors.[1]

---

1. Viggo Søgaard, *Media in Church and Mission, Communicating the Gospel.* William Carey Library, 1993:229–232, for a description of the process.

DECISION-MAKING AND RESEARCH

In order to decide on a proper research function, we need, of course, to understand the specific context in which it will be used. We can think of a number of possibilities, such as selling books or Bibles, conducting youth camps, leading churches into growth, radio broadcasting, service to communities, seminaries and Bible schools, Sunday schools, mission to unreached groups, community development, literacy training, video and cassette production, and so on.

When considering research in church and mission, it is, therefore, helpful to begin by asking questions such as:

1. *What type of ministry is involved?*
2. *What kind of leadership is being utilized?*
3. *What kind of information would help them perform better?*
4. *What is the present role of research in the organization?*

There are many variables in the decision-making process to which research relates. Some of these variables can be controlled, others are variables in the context or environment over which we have no control, but we can understand them through research and then adapt our strategy to such conditions.

The following diagram, figure 1.1, illustrates this situation. Our ministry activities can be controlled. These are issues like the program itself and the products we produce, promotional activities and publicity material, pricing of products and services, and the people involved in the activity.

The contextual factors which we cannot control will include such issues as the national religion, the local economic situation, the prevailing political situation, the educational level of the audience, and the needs of the audience.

The direct results we will be seeking may be sales of Bible portions, people attending an event, or letters from listeners, but our real results should be increased knowledge of the word of God, change in belief, and actual behavioral changes.

The results can, in turn, be measured by observable results such as letters or response cards, or through some kind of research methodology.

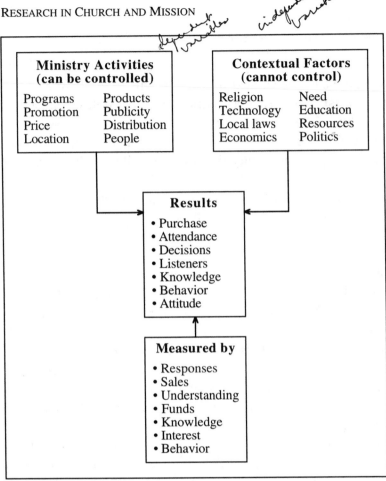

Figure 1. 1
Measuring Ministry Results

THE MANAGEMENT PROCESS TO WHICH RESEARCH RELATES

Let us briefly look at the management-decision process itself. Most leaders make many decisions every day. Obviously, extensive research is not practical for routine decisions, and most of these are taken at a moment's notice. They will follow a usual pattern for the church or the organization, drawing on ongoing information and monitoring. Survey research primarily comes in when special situations occur. This may be falling membership, or it may be the planning of a crusade or a new outreach program in the inner city. There is a certain sequence to such a decision-making process:

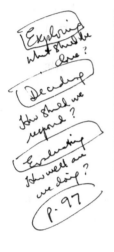

1. *Realize the Need for a Decision*
2. *Define the Decision Problem*
3. *Identify Possible Solutions*
4. *Evaluate Alternatives*
5. *Select an Approach*
6. *Implementation and Action*

Figure 1. 2
Management Decision Process

1. *Realize that a problem exits or that new possibilities are available.* Both of these, the present problem and the opening of new possibilities, can be due to changes in environmental factors. It could be members moving to the suburbs from the area surrounding the church. The problems or the possibilities may also grow out of a change in the general objectives of the organization. In any case, the leadership is faced with a decision to solve the problem at hand, and this may in turn lead to new growth.

2. *Define the decision that needs to be reached.* It is important to identify the key issues involved, and the factors that influence the situation as well as the decision possibilities. Often help is needed at this stage, and an outsider can help as a consultant. A well-functioning research system may prove to be invaluable.

3. *Identify the possible alternative solutions.* We are often hindered by our previous approaches and the ways we used to do things. In Christian ministry we have seen many approaches that are applied universally, or organizations that work on "one-kind solutions." But new situations demand new answers, so a creative process of brainstorming, followed by a narrowing of realistic alternatives, will be extremely important.

4. *Evaluate the alternatives.* If quick decisions are mandatory, the immediate evaluation of alternatives by the management team may

be an acceptable course of action. On the other hand, if time is available, the research department can help by pretesting alternative solutions or approaches to the situation. This will reduce the risk for wrong decisions and waste of resources. One alternative may be to do nothing.

5. *Select an approach.* Decisions are reached on the basis of available information, previous experience, intuition and what we could call inner peace. When a decision is reached, it will need to be communicated to all who will be benefited by knowing it, or will/can help solve the problem.

6. *Implementation and action.* A decision has been taken, a course of action pointed out. This will be followed by an action plan and the necessary budget allocation. Again, research should be involved in monitoring the progress, so that information is constantly available for reviewing decisions.

In such a management-decision process, the research function is available at all steps to provide the information needed by the leadership. It is not just a question of collecting data, but of selecting and interpreting data that provide information on how to solve the problem at hand. If the research department is not involved in the decision-making process, they will most likely provide data for which there is no use or no interpretation. The gathering of data can then be a very useless activity. By being involved in the process, the researcher will turn the data into valuable information that will help the leadership set proper objectives, plan the ministry, and monitor the results.

SCOPE OF COMMUNICATION RESEARCH

The scope of communication research has been well stated by Lasswell in his famous sentence on the effects of communication. Communication effects depend on,

Lasswell identified five elements, and each of these five elements can be researched. We need an information system that will gather information on the communicator, the content, the media, the audience, and the impact.

Who Says What
To Whom
In Which Channel
With What Effect

Figure 1. 3
Lasswell's Model[2]

Another approach would be to look at the function of research in the following broad categories:

1. **Our approach:** The study will focus on the mix of the components of our ministry, that is, cost factors, facilities, publicity, and general promotion, which are all factors or variables we can control. A mix of these elements will form the strategy we use to achieve our goals. Research will help us decide how to combine them.

2. **The context:** This is a study of the environment in which we function. The context and surroundings in which we work consist of what can be called independent variables, that is, variables we do not or cannot control. These include factors such as general economic environment, competition from both religious and secular organizations, the local media situation, fashion and trends, legal constraints, and top news stories. Our controllable variables will need to function within the context of such independent variables.

3. **The response:** Our intention is to achieve behavioral responses from the audience. This may be a change in life-style, purchase of a Bible, a change in attitude toward church, belief in Christ, or a decision to give ten dollars to a mission cause. We could call these dependent variables, which are greatly influenced by a person's previous information and experience with the topic or issue. A good approach or communication strategy will be supported by a

---

2. Wilbur Schramm and Donald F. Roberts, *The Process and Effects of Mass Communication*. University of Illinois Press, Second Edition, 1971:84.

research system that provides information on how the listener or reader handles information. Ongoing monitoring of sales, listenership, image, response, etc. will provide information on long-term trends.

Most likely, research will not provide all the answers, and it will not give the whole picture. Consequently, management will also need to include a dependence on previous experience and intuition. For the Christian, a dependence on the guidance of the Spirit will provide the "intuition" or peace that a leader will need in his or her decision-making task. Research will aid by providing information for that task.

THE FIELD OF COMMUNICATION RESEARCH

Our information system will usually draw on the insights and methodologies obtained from various academic disciplines. Consequently, communication research can be seen as an applied science that draws on other fields of study and research: anthropology, sociology, marketing, as well as media research. The methodologies are similar, yet influenced by the specific interests and demands of a particular academic discipline. In the following, we shall look briefly at some of these disciplines and their usefulness for communication research.

Marketing Research

Kinnear and Taylor define marketing research as *"the systematic and objective approach to the development and provision of information for the marketing management decision-making process."*[3] Much of the material in this book will be based on insights from marketing research.

From the above definition, we can identify four key words about marketing research:[4] (1) it is a *systematic activity*, that is well organized and planned. It will require a researcher who understands the methods used

---

3. The following points are adapted from Thomas C. Kinnear and James R. Taylor, *Marketing Research, An Applied Approach.* McGraw-Hill, Fourth Edition, 1991:6.
4. Ibid., pp. 6–7.

and is capable of carrying out the necessary activities with great care and attention to details. (2) It is an *objective activity*, a scientific exercise where all efforts will be made to avoid bias and emotions. The researcher will need to be able to keep distance and objectivity, even when the data may show discouraging signs. (3) It is the *provision of information* that will relate to a specific situation. Information is data interpreted in the perspective of the needs of our present situation and decision-making problem. Finally, (4) it is *research for decision-making*. These last two points make a marketing approach to research different from anthropological research where anything of interest may be counted. In a marketing approach to research, we only count what needs to be counted, and all research activities are directly concerned with the application of findings into actual ministry. (There are, though, also basic marketing research studies, or fundamental research where we are aiming at extending our basic knowledge).

As the marketing concept is adopted by more and more organizations, including service and nonprofit organizations such as Bible societies, the understanding of the nature and role of marketing research has expanded. Marketing research has developed extensive methodologies and techniques for the actual collection of data, and it is primarily from marketing research that we obtain the necessary tools for survey research, which is a primary methodology used by communication researchers.

A primary concern in this book, then, is survey research, and this will begin by clearly identifying the purpose of a research project. To arrive at good definitions of purpose, both the researcher and the management/ leadership will need to be involved. Following the development of research objectives, the next question concerns the information needed. A list of specific information needs is designed to guide the development of the questionnaire and other aspects of the study and it will help in the interpretation of collected data. Careful preparation of objectives and information needs will save time and money later, and it will avoid the collection of unnecessary data.

Anthropological Research

Survey research is especially helpful for gathering information that can be quantified, but for other areas of communication research and for the purpose of analyzing a people's worldview, we can learn from the principles of anthropological research. Anthropological research distinguishes between the following methods of study.[5]

Participant Observation. Here the researcher will take up residence in the community, and detailed data are obtained by observations. Producers of Christian radio programs can follow the same approach as they try to understand their listeners, possibly living in a community for a period. A friend of this writer once became a shepherd for a week to prepare himself for making programs for shepherds and their families.

Key-Informant Interviewing. The researcher will use "key informants" as sources of information about their own cultures. Similarly, Christian communicators can conduct regular in-depth interviews with selected people representing the group they are trying to communicate with. This may even be a neighbor.

Collection of Life Histories. Such stories can often serve the researcher in his or her study of how past events have an effect on present beliefs and values. Testimonies of individuals, mapping their life-history, can help us understand the background to their present attitudes and understanding, as well as help us design strategies for reaching others like them.

Structured Interviews. In this much more structured phase of a research project, a representative sample is studied to provide quantification. This is similar to survey research, but will often be done with a much smaller sample of respondents.

Projective Techniques. A number of different techniques can be used, for example sentence-completion techniques. A person is asked to complete a sentence such as, "I would consider becoming a Christian, if . . ." Such a procedure will often give clues to their real felt needs and attitudes.

Unobtrusive Measures. This refers to situations where the people studied are not aware that an analysis is going on. It may be analyzing responses to a ministry on the basis of follow-up cards, or just to listen as they tune their radios to the music they like.

Through such methodologies and techniques, anthropological research can provide significant data on media communication, and most impor-

---

5.   For a study of anthropological research the following two books can be recommended: Pertti J. Pelto and Gretel H. Pelto, *Anthropological Research, The Structure of Inquiry*. Cambridge University Press, Second Edition, 1978. James P. Spradley, *Participant Observation*. Holt, Rinehart and Winston, 1980.

tantly, provide media programmers with information on how to establish communication with a particular group of people. Their reading habits can be observed to know how important reading is to them. Their felt needs, their interests, and their daily concerns can be uncovered by a researcher who actually lives among the people.

Intercultural Research   *take intercultural understanding —*

Intercultural research is not a methodology like marketing or anthropological research but should be understood as the applied area of adapting and using research methodologies and principles in intercultural settings.

Outside highly developed industrial countries, marketing research data and studies are very few, and many approaches developed in the West may not be suitable. Anthropological researchers have, on the other hand, primarily worked in so-called developing countries, and they have usually worked with research measures other than those using probability sampling. Western-developed approaches to probability sampling are often impossible in intercultural settings, so great creativity is needed. This does not imply that such sampling cannot be carried out, but it does mean that new and creative adaptations are often needed.

The question of data quality control in intercultural surveys should always be taken seriously, as errors in the data can completely distort the results of an analysis. It is our experience from studies in Asian countries that a stratified probability sample is possible and very useful. Panels with self-administered questionnaires have also proved helpful. Similarly, group interviews with individual, anonymous, self-administered questionnaires have worked well. On the other hand, non-probability samples are often more realistic, and a carefully planned quota sample may in many situations be more practical and representative. A researcher with proper training in research methodology as well as in cultural anthropology should be able to work out designs that give reliable data.

THE RESEARCH PROCESS

To conduct a survey research project, we need a fairly long process as illustrated in figure 1.4. It begins by defining the need for information and then gives a careful description of research objectives. This will, in turn, be followed by the development of a list of information needs, the kind of information that we will need to meet our objectives. We then need to decide from whom we need this information. On the basis of that we can develop a research design and sampling plan.

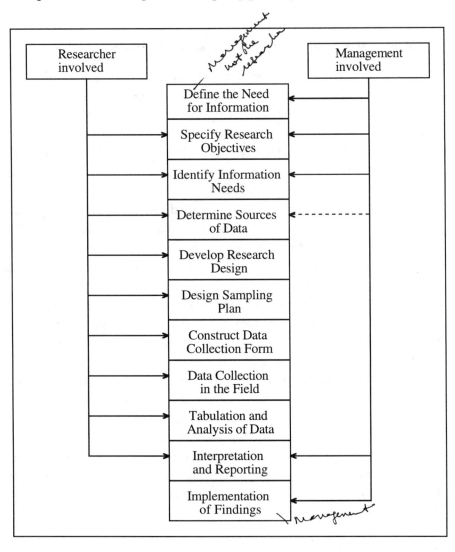

Figure 1. 4
The Survey Research Process

Only when all of the above has been carried out will we be able to construct the questionnaire, which is the form on which we collect the data. Details will also need to be worked out to provide instruction for field workers. Finally comes the work of tabulation, interpretation and reporting. Hopefully, the management will then be able to phase the findings into applied strategy.

Where Can We Go Wrong? *every step.*

Research is a science where attention must be paid to details and procedures if reliable information is to be obtained. All too often we hear Christian leaders give negative remarks regarding statistics. The problem is not the use of statistics, but the wrong use or misuse of statistics. The steps and procedures outlined in this book are aimed at reducing error and making research findings valuable and reliable.

There are two basic types of error: sampling error and non-sampling error. Sampling error is error associated with the selection of the respondents in a sample. Statistics are based on samples of the population, and the errors associated with sampling can be measured and decreased as the sample size increases.

Non-sampling errors are all other kinds of error associated with the research process. Most of our study of research relates to how we can reduce non-sampling error. A first step is to realize its existence and where it can occur, and what effects error can have on the results of a study. Then we develop the skills that will help us to reduce it to the lowest possible level. Non-sampling error cannot be measured, and most likely it will increase as sample size increases.

Among the many possible causes of error in the research process, the following should be noted: (1) inadequate description of the need for this specific research project; (2) research objectives too vague, resulting in vague formulation of information needs; (3) the research design itself may be flawed; (4) sampling plan may have problems, (5) poorly constructed questionnaire or significant bias; (6) measurement error, including the use of wrong statistics; (7) interviewer-related errors; (8) tabulation error; and (9) misinterpreting or misusing the data. For reliable and valid research, we must do what we can to avoid such errors.

A FEW ETHICAL QUESTIONS

In a research project, we gain significant insight into such areas as a person's life-style, tastes, and needs. The interview process itself is a communication process, where you communicate with a respondent in order to obtain certain information. A high level of trust has to be present, or there will be no cooperation. This makes the respondent vulnerable and an easy target of manipulation. It is our obligation to treat the information correctly and protect the respondent from public misrepresentation or exploitation. Consequently, both ethical standards and laws have been worked out governing research work. Ethical standards will make certain types of activities inappropriate.

Generally speaking, research must not be used to trick a person in order to sell a product, including a religious product or faith. For example, the use of a questionnaire to gain entrance into a home in order to "evangelize" the respondent is highly questionable from an ethics perspective, and may actually be illegal according to the laws of the country. A number of codes of ethics have been worked out by interested organizations.

LEGAL QUESTIONS

Apart from ethical questions, we also need to consider legal aspects. For the Christian researcher, the ethical issues raised above should be sufficient, but we need to underline that the respective authorities view misuse of research and exploitation of the respondents with seriousness. We can, for example, mention that in the United States, the Federal Trade Commission has successfully taken legal action against organizations using research as a trick to solicit sales. There has also been action against firms that used research data to develop mailing lists for direct-mail schemes. Legal action has also been taken against companies that stated that research data was free from all non-sampling error.[6]

Let us just remind ourselves that improper use of research methods and the misrepresentation of data is, at least in some cases, a criminal activity. Christian organizations should never compromise ethical codes or legal issues related to research, even when done under the cover of evangelism.

---

6. Thomas C. Kinnear and James R. Taylor, *Marketing Research, An Applied Approach.* McGraw-Hill, Fourth Edition, 1991:57–59.

For Research Users, Practitioners, and Interviewers

1. No individual or organization will undertake any activity which is directly or indirectly represented to be marketing research, but which has as its real purpose the attempted sale of merchandise or services to some or all of the respondents interviewed in the course of the research.
2. If a respondent has been led to believe, directly or indirectly, that he is participating in a marketing research survey and that his anonymity will be protected, his name shall not be made known to anyone outside the research organization or research department, or used for other than research purposes.

For Research Practitioners

1. There will be no intentional or deliberate misrepresentation of research methods or results. An adequate description of methods employed will be made available upon request to the sponsor of the research. Evidence that field work has been completed according to specifications will, upon request, be made available to buyers of research.
2. The identity of the survey sponsor and/or the ultimate client for whom a survey is being done will be held in confidence at times, unless this identity is to be revealed as part of the research design. Research information shall be held in confidence by the research organization or department and not used for personal gain or made available to any outside party unless the client specifically authorizes such release.
3. A research organization shall not undertake marketing studies for competitive clients when such studies would jeopardize the confidential nature of client-agency relationships.

For Users of Marketing Research

1. A user of research shall not knowingly disseminate conclusions from a given research project or service that are inconsistent with or not warranted by the data.
2. To the extent that there is involved in a research project a unique design involving techniques, approaches, or concepts not commonly available to research practitioners, the prospective user of research shall not solicit such a design from one practitioner and deliver it to another for execution without the approval of the design originator.

For Field Interviewers

1. Research assignments and materials received, as well as information obtained from respondents, shall be held in confidence by the interviewer and revealed to no one except the research organization conducting the marketing study.
2. No information gained through a marketing research activity shall be used, directly or indirectly, for the personal gain or advantage of the interviewer.
3. Interviews shall be conducted in strict accordance with specifications and instructions received.
4. An interviewer shall not carry out two or more interviewing assignments simultaneously unless authorized by all contractors or employees concerned.

Members of American Marketing Association will be expected to conduct themselves in accordance with the provisions of this Code in all of their marketing research activities.

Figure 1. 5
American Marketing Association's
Marketing Research Code of Ethics[7]

---

7. Ibid., p. 53–54.

2

RESEARCH AND APPLIED COMMUNICATION

This book treats research in the context of Christian communication, so a brief introduction to communication principles is provided in this chapter. As such, the chapter provides a framework for the conceptualization of research purpose and objectives.

The term communication has been understood in a variety of ways, depending on the background and experience of the people concerned. For some, communication is fund-raising, and for others it is publicity. For many, the word communication equals "media." But even for the media people, the term is used differently. We can conclude, though, that all Christian media people and others involved in ministry will need to grasp communication principles in order to produce good materials and programs.

Christian communication has a number of special dimensions and is influenced by certain constant and variable factors that not only set it apart, but also make it superior to any other kind of communication.[1] This is primarily due to the fact that God is the God who communicates with humanity. Communication is deeply rooted in God's nature, and it is this

---

1. Knud Jørgensen, *The Role and Function of the Media in the Mission of the Church.* Unpublished Ph.D. dissertation presented to Fuller Theological Seminary, School of World Mission, Pasadena, 1981.

nature he imparted to humanity when he created us in his own image. Communication is therefore not something accidental or supplementary for human beings, but it is the only way to be fully human. Furthermore, God has given us a mandate to communicate a message to others (Mt. 28:18–20). All of this, in turn, makes special demands on the use of communication research methodologies.

Many problems encountered in the evangelistic and missionary enterprise of the church arise from the failure to distinguish between constant and variable factors. Constants are the basic, fundamental aspects that should always be kept in mind, and it is the foundation on which we stand. Constant factors that never change include the commission to communicate, the opposing evil forces, and the work of the Spirit. Variables are factors that do change, and they provide the environment of our communication and influence the form and the content of our messages. The variables are, then, the primary focus of communication research, and later in this chapter we will look closer at some of them.

GOD IS A COMMUNICATOR

God is by nature a communicator. There are many attributes of God we will never be able to understand or fully comprehend, but through a study of the Scriptures, and by analyzing results of his dealings with people, we can learn much about his communication methods. He "expressed" himself at the time of Creation. He spoke, and things happened, and from the creation of the world, God has been communicating (revealing) himself to humanity. He sought company with Adam, Abraham, Moses, and David. He let his Son live in a social context, and he leads his people into a warm community of believers. When looking at the way in which he communicates, we can learn significant lessons and develop models for Christian communication. Also, by looking at God's concerns, we should be able to evaluate the effects of Christian communication from the perspective of God.

In the following, we will look at some of the dimensions that are of special importance in God's communicational activities.[2]

---

2.   Charles H. Kraft, *Communication Theory for Christian Witness*. Maryknoll, NY: Orbis Books, Rev. Ed., 1991.

God Makes Himself Known

From the creation of the world God has been communicating (revealing) himself to humanity. Creation is one of the vehicles through which God speaks, and the Bible is the record of that communication. The Church is the living voice through which he continues to speak to the world. In the Old Testament we see God communicating through acts and words, through the universe he created and through history as well as through special revelation. Israel knew God through their history (Rom. 1:20; Ps. 19:1–4). In the New Testament God reveals himself fully through his Son. In him God is present, incarnated (Heb. 1:1–3a; 1 Cor. 2:10).

The incarnation of Jesus sets the stage for perfect communication between God and humanity. It is the climax of God's communication with us. "The Son is the radiance of God's glory and the exact representation of his being" (Heb. 1:3) and "the image of the invisible God" (Col. 1:15). When the disciples wanted to see the Father, Jesus said, in effect, Look at me (John 14:8ff). Jesus spoke the words the Father sent him to speak (John 3:34), and he carried out the work of the Father (John 10:37–38). The lesson for the Christian communicator is to be completely identified with the message preached. Through research we can discover how true this is of our communication.

God Wants to be Understood

God wants to be understood correctly so that the appropriate response can be obtained. He therefore uses communication symbols that are understood by us within our specific cultural contexts. He uses language, culture, and human form.[3] In his communication, he is not out to impress us, as we so often seem tempted to do in our sermons. In God's communication, the impressiveness is in the content of his message[4] and not in the form or method of communication. Jesus might have been more impressive if he had spoken in Hebrew, or even in Greek, but he used Aramaic, the common language of the people so that they might understand. Our Christian rituals and services may be very impressive, but do they communicate meaning to the average member of the congregation?

---

3. Ibid.
4. Ibid., p. 21.

God is teaching us that understanding must be our primary concern, and through our research we will usually want to see if we have achieved understanding with our audience. We need to study the use and meaning of communication signals, including the use and meaning of words.

God Wants a Relationship

The fall of humanity can be seen primarily as a breakdown in communication. When Adam ran away from God, he not only ran away from communion and dialogue with God, but he also caused a breakdown in other areas of communication.[5] Apart from a breakdown of communication with God, there was disruption within the person, peace was broken among people, and there was a breakdown of communication and relationship with the created universe (Gen. 3:8, 4:12, 6:5, 11:4, 3:17–20, 4:11,14). But God yearns to be known and this yearning makes him wrestle with Israel again and again. He yearns to be in a true relationship with each one of us. Jesus taught us to seek relationships with those we try to reach.

In our research we will need to infer the relationship a person has with God from observed behavior, including Bible study, prayer, and worship attendance.

God Wants a Response

God does not seem to be happy with a passive response but seeks an interactive relationship. In dealing with us, he uses a variety of methods to achieve an active response. It may be a question, as with Adam. Jesus told parables where the listeners became players in a drama. An active response to God implies commitment. Kraft suggests that this commitment have at least three dimensions:[6] (a) As the Head of the church, Christ commits himself to us, his body (Eph. 5:24–25) and we, in turn, are to respond by commitment to him, our Head. (b) As members of a body, God desires that we commit ourselves to each other (1 Cor. 12:12ff; Eph.

---

5.   Robert E. Webber, *God Still Speaks: A Biblical View of Christian Communication.* Thomas Nelson Publishers, 1980:115ff.
6.   Charles E. Kraft, *Communication Theory for Christian Witness.* Maryknoll, NY: Orbis Books, Rev. Ed., 1991:19.

5:21). (c) God intends that we share his commitment with the world at large (John 21:21).

Christians have often been satisfied with only measuring immediate responses to a message, or what can be seen as surface measures. If we are to follow God's example in our communication, it will be much more important for us to measure long-term changes and real commitment than just the raising of hands.

The Incarnation is His Primary Method   *Receptive orientation*

When we look at God's incarnation, we are looking at the center of communication, and the essential essence of communication theory. Through the incarnation, God was bending down[7] to disclose himself through ordinary situations of human life, thus becoming completely relevant to the context of human beings. He did it at a particular time in history and through one particular culture. By studying this incarnational communication of God, we will not refute human communication, but discover the key that can redeem or restore the human communication process.[8]

The incarnation is then the ideal model of communication. It is the crowning event in which all other forms of God's communication with humanity are embodied. Communication through incarnation is being involved in a context, entering into the real problems, issues, and struggles of the people. Jesus did not just speak to the Jews, but he became a Jew and identified himself with all aspects of Jewish life. He identified with the social outcasts and participated in the social relationships of the Jewish culture. He became a true human being, even working as a carpenter. He spoke to their particular needs, rather than presenting a message of universal abstracts.

In a recent study conducted by faculty members and graduate students from Fuller Seminary School of World Mission, it is clear that when an incarnational model is attempted, the response is much higher.[9] An incarnational model demands that the messengers live among the people they serve.

---

7. Charles H. Kraft, *Christianity in Culture*. Maryknoll, NY: Orbis Books, 1979:210.
8. Knud Jørgensen, *The Role and Function of the Media in the Mission of the Church*. Unpublished Ph.D. dissertation presented to Fuller Theological Seminary, School of World Mission, Pasadena, 1981:27.

A COMMISSION TO COMMUNICATE

As Christian communicators we are entering into the ministry which has been God's concern through the ages: revealing him to humanity. This commission to communicate permeates all aspects of Christian ministry, and it is the motivational force for commitment and dedication. This "communication for a purpose" is always present in the Scriptures. God communicated himself to the prophets and then commissioned them to be his communicators to others. He communicated himself—in fullness—through the Son and then commissioned the Son to a ministry (Heb. 1:1–3). Christ communicated with the apostles and then commissioned them as communicators (Mt. 28:18–20). Today those who have experienced his revelation are called to be his ambassadors representing and communicating him in the world (2 Cor. 5:20). How well the church has lived up to, or rather failed to live up to the commission given by Christ is clearly evident in the world today. The great majority of the earth's population have yet to become followers of Jesus Christ.

Our Task is Communication

Communication is implied in the words of John 20:21, "As the Father has sent me, so I send you." Christ is sending us to represent him, and to communicate him by his standards and his methods. The church has not always understood the implications and responsibilities inherent in this commission, and has often failed to communicate the message to others.

Central to the Christian communication process is the use of words, but, just because a person listens to certain words does not guarantee that he or she understands the words the same way as the speaker and that the true meaning is achieved. Words in themselves have no magic. Just because a person says that he believes in God does not necessarily mean that he believes in God, the creator of the universe and the Father of our Lord Jesus Christ. It may signify a belief in some kind of cosmic force, or even in self. The Buddhist will use many of the same terms and words as the Christian, but with drastically different meanings and connotations.

---

9.   Confidential research report on Movement in Bangladesh. Submitted by Fuller
     Theological Seminary and Global Partners for Development, 1995.

The Muslim will be closer to the Christian understanding, but again different meanings are associated with the same words.

The implications for the pastor of a local church, as well as for the radio speaker, will be to study the use of words and the connotations that the congregation and listeners associate with the words, and here research methods can provide significant help. We need to choose the words that will create the right meaning in their minds. Otherwise, communication will be a wishful dream rather than a reality. Careful research into what has actually been communicated is important for future planning.

Our Method of Communication

God achieved his communicational goals through love. He is a true lover,[10] and he demonstrated that to be a true lover is to have as our primary concern the needs of the receptors without considering the cost to ourselves.[11] In other words, God's approach is receptor-oriented communication. Such an approach demands a high respect for the receptors (the audience), a trust in them as persons created in the image of God, and even making ourselves vulnerable in our communication. It also means entering totally into the context of the audience, using their language and frame of reference. In his incarnation, Jesus showed us the perfect example of such an approach.

The implications of such a position are far-reaching for Christian communicators. Have we devoted all our efforts to refining the packaging without examining the product? Is it legitimate to broadcast Bible studies produced in Europe or America on radio stations all round Asia and Africa and argue that the one gospel has been faithfully communicated to all these cultures? A lot of research is waiting to be done to get a clear picture of the results of such programs.

Or, do we, for example, show concern for the other person when the Scriptures are only available in print for a people who are primarily non-literate? Analysis of effective communication methods and media is still needed.

---

10. Em Griffin, *The Mind Changers*. Tyndale House, 1976.
11. Charles H. Kraft, *Communication Theory for Christian Witness*. Maryknoll, NY: Orbis Books, Rev.Ed., 1991:23.

Our Communication Message

The essential content of all aspects of evangelism is Bible teaching, centering around Jesus Christ. The message of the Bible is addressed to all humans, and through it the Holy Spirit still speaks today. The apostle Paul exhorted Timothy to continue in what he had learned and firmly believed, that "Scripture is inspired by God and profitable for teaching, for reproof, for correction, and for training in righteousness, that the man of God may be complete, equipped for every good work" (2 Tim. 3:14–17).

Jesus spent much of his time with his small group of disciples, but a significant amount of time was also spent communicating with the multitudes, or we could say with mass audiences and large crowds. His "program" then included plenty of stories (which we call parables), stories they could understand and in which they saw themselves as actors in a drama. He demonstrated his power to them by healing the sick and casting out the demons. He fed the thousands who had nothing to eat, and he confronted the power structures with prophetic announcements. In many ways, the kind of things on which we build our media programs and popular sermons. But when Jesus was alone with his disciples, he taught them "theory." He explained the meanings of things and how the various items fitted together in a conceptual framework. Likewise, those of us who are engaged in the ministry as pastors of churches, as missiologists, or media practitioners, need to step back and understand what we are doing. We need to utilize the created ability to conceptualize and theorize, to work with symbols and signs, and to arrange concepts into theories that help us understand and visualize processes. In other words, we need to be concerned about the theories and principles on which our ministry is carried out.

Jesus was bringing the Kingdom of God and in his kingdom, the atmosphere is *Shalom*. Our goal will therefore be to restore true peace in all our relationships: relationship with God (theology), peace and wholeness within people (psychology), peace and good relationships among men and women (sociology), and a true relationship with the created universe (ecology). As he leads us into community with his people in the church, he also restores a new kind of bond among us (ecclesiology). As we shall see later, research methodologies are available for studying the effects of Christian communication from such a perspective.

THE CHANGING CONTEXT

In downtown areas of cities around the world we find churches sitting on extremely valuable real estate but without viable congregations. The churches were built when people lived in the city, or at least those who attended church lived in the city and close to the church. Today, the immediate context of the church has changed. It may now be a business area with high-rise office buildings, or it may be a low cost housing estate or even a slum area, and many of the church-goers live in suburbs and drive in to church on Sunday morning. The people who live in the surrounding areas are usually not seen in their "neighborhood church." We need to study why this is so, and what is needed to make them interested in coming inside.

Similar observations can be made of some Christian media programs. Program format, music selections, content, and way of presentation all seem to speak to certain sectors of the society, that is, those who are already believers and live in comfortable surroundings. Rarely do we hear programs that are geared to the needs of the poor, the homeless, or the outcasts. A purely verbal gospel does not seem to have the answers for their situation.

Changing contexts demand variety in approaches to communication, so we shall look at some variable factors that are of special interest to Christian communication. By identifying these factors, we should be able to handle them without too much uncertainty, and then develop realistic and relevant approaches. For each situation, careful research will be called for.

The Cultural Context

A culture defines, to a large extent, a people's way of life, their institutions and structures. This should also apply to the church planted within a new culture. Its structures, and patterns of leadership, worship and church life should be congenial to its people. Unfortunately, this has not always been true, and we have churches that only faintly mirror the surrounding culture. This gives the church an almost impossible situation as far as communication and image is concerned.

The cultural issue was faced by the apostle Paul in his time and ministry. For a considerable period he battled the efforts of a Judaizing sect within the church to require non-Jews to observe Jewish cultural norms and forms. Paul resisted this because of his respect for cultural diversity and because he realized that in order to communicate effectively with all people, he had to become "all things to all" (1 Cor. 9:22).

From our study of Scripture and cultural anthropology we must conclude that it is the communicator who must change his or her patterns to fit the cultural context of the receptor audience. The communicator must, therefore, study the culture of the audience to see how the gospel of Christ can be communicated within that frame of reference.

Society in Which We Live

In contemporary society, we tend to forget that society is a variable factor that constantly changes. Our understanding of society varies and the words that describe social and political factors change in meaning. This is partly due to our upbringing and to the specific society in which we live. A Social Democrat from Denmark may, for example, view social issues as much more crucial to biblical Christianity than a Republican American does. Much of what is seen to be "Christian" or not to be "Christian" is strongly influenced by our society and its norms. A society will also prescribe its own use of media channels and media content, providing different media situations from country to country.

Cultures and societies change from one period of time to another. The tendency is to assume that activities, forms, and methods that were relevant in a past era are equally relevant everywhere and for all times. Examples would be hymns, or particular versions of the Bible. We need to study the effects of such approaches and how communication and understanding can be achieved.

The Spiritual Position of the Receptor

People are not all at the same stage in their intellectual or spiritual understanding and development. Some individuals are like "fields ripe for harvest," other "fields" need to be cleared of weeds and thistles, even before "gospel-sowing" can take place. Gibbs reminds us that the hard ground of the path, as described in the parable of the sower, represents ground made hard by other people's feet.[12] Such hard ground may of itself be good soil, but it is made seemingly unreceptive by a variety of influences that need to be understood. Careful research can uncover the underlying tensions.

In chapter three we shall be dealing with this issue of spiritual process in much more depth, so at this time we only need to remind ourselves that as the spiritual position and background of the receptor changes, so will the need arise to select and adapt one's communication content and approach. Research methodologies are available for studying the spiritual position of a person.

The Personality and Gifts of the Communicator

Christ has prepared all of us for ministry. He has done so through a unique and creative process (1 Pet. 1:2) which includes our social context and education, and the training we have received. Furthermore, he has prepared us by giving spiritual gifts (1 Cor. 12:4ff). The purpose has been to prepare us for ministry. So like the apostle Paul, we are given extensive "equipment" for ministry: natural talents, upbringing and education, life experiences and specific spiritual gifts.

As Christians are diverse in temperament and background, their manner and methods of communication will likewise be varied. We should accept this diversity as a blessing, knowing that God can both bless and use all of us and a wide variety of approaches. Change in methods and media is necessary if we are to use our gifts to the fullest and turn our attention from the medium to the person.

A method-bound movement cannot become an effective world movement, but it will soon be relegated to the outdated and the outworn. Just because a method has proved to be useful in one context does not mean it will be equally useful in other contexts. Unfortunately, the world of Christian ministry is swamped by "copyrighted" methods and products that often do not fit the personality and gifts of the communicator who attempts to use them.

---

12. Eddie Gibbs, *The God Who Communicates*. Hodder and Stoughton, 1985:39.

THE OPPOSING FORCES

As long as we live in this age, our task of communicating the Word of God will meet with hostility and obstruction from the powers of evil. The apostle Paul gave clear teaching on this. These powers of evil have blinded the minds of those who do not believe and they can apparently also directly stop or obstruct the Christian mission. Paul experienced this in his ministry, but he found that there are ways to overcome such evil powers (1 Thess. 2:18 and 3:1f). Christ is stronger, and he gives his servants wisdom, power, and endurance.

The Christian communicator may find the ministry hindered by seemingly unnecessary roadblocks. We may tend to call such obstruction communication failures, but they may also be caused by the powers of darkness. Or, attacks may come in the form of temptations, aimed at destroying Christian leaders. As long as nothing happens, we are not dangerous, but when effective ministry is experienced, then we also see the problems and obstacles caused by the evil one.

Another obstacle to communication is the fallen nature of the human race which is in rebellion against God (Rom. 1:18); people do not seek God and are not interested in understanding God.

THE WORK OF THE SPIRIT

Christian communication is a spiritual work, and, ultimately, all results will depend on the Holy Spirit. In the task of proclaiming the gospel, the Spirit utilizes the church as his agent, but the task of bringing a person from darkness into the light of Christ is the exclusive role of the Holy Spirit (John 6:44; Titus 3:5–7). The communicator is a witness and a channel, not the power.

It is the Spirit who truly controls the whole process of gospel communication. We are told in 1 Corinthians 2:1–16 that the Spirit enables us to "know," "speak," "interpret," and "judge" or "appraise" spiritual truths. Thus the constant power source is the Holy Spirit. The "communication link" is prayer (Eph. 6:18–20). The implications for the Christian communicator is to commit himself or herself through prayer to the guidance of the Spirit and then anticipate the mighty work of the Spirit in conviction and healing, and in the creation of true wholeness.

This involvement by the Spirit is not a "cooperative effort" by God and human beings, as if there are areas and capacities of our lives outside his control. It is not a question of God and me each making a contribution, but rather, it is a question of the indwelling Christ working through his body, the church, and its individual members. It is an incarnational concept, Christ in us, working through us (Col. 1:27).

We sometimes see references made to the "part" played by the Holy Spirit. This would seem to imply that we are "using" the Spirit, rather than the Spirit using us. Christ is not only using us, and speaking through us as his ambassadors (2 Cor. 5:20), but he is also working through the mental capacities he has given us to develop plans and carry out communicational activities. In the language of communication, Christ is encoded in our lives, making it essential that we, the communicators, are part of the message we communicate.

Faith relates to the work of the Spirit. Christianity is a religion of faith, and Christian communication must be carried out in faith (Heb. 11). It is through the eyes of faith that we see God; and without faith, no spiritual work can be carried out. Salvation is received by faith, and the Christian life is lived in and by faith. For the Christian communicator "faith" is more than dreams or wishful thinking. It is a conviction based on the calling of Christ. It is the "confident assurance that something we want is going to happen." And it is "the certainty that what we hope for is waiting for us, even though we cannot see it up ahead" (Heb. 11:1 LB). The communicator will, therefore, often continue ministry in spite of what seems to be impossibilities. Faith gives hope. In chapter three we will be dealing with strategy and goal setting, but let us remind ourselves at this point that any goal setting in Christian ministry is, to use Dayton's terminology, "statements of faith."[13] In prayer we seek the mind of the Lord, depending on his Spirit for guidance. Then in his power we go forth.

The work of the Spirit challenges and humbles the Christian researcher. We cannot research how the Spirit will work or where, and we cannot predict the results of spiritual work through the application of statistics. Only God knows, but he does use us and he wants us to be accountable servants. The temptation will of course be to take credit for

---

13. Edward R. Dayton and David A. Fraser, *Planning Strategies for World Evangelization.* 2nd edition, MARC, 1990:14.

results that are not due to us. This, in turn, makes special demands on the researcher who is studying the effects of ministry.

THE EFFECTS OF COMMUNICATION

Our Lord did not set a time frame for our fulfilling the great commission. The task of making disciples of all nations, tribes and people will be a constant as long as this age lasts. On the other hand, Jesus would probably not give such a commission if the goal was not obtainable. Christian communicators will, therefore, always work towards this goal and they will not be content with just "participatory" communication or dialogue. A Christian will communicate for impact, or for the purpose of achieving certain effects.

In measuring the effects of Christian communication, we often encounter so-called spiritual and theological objections. Some Christian groups will object to the use of research on the basis of a conviction that it is unnecessary for the Christian—who relies on the Holy Spirit—to ask questions concerning effectiveness. Others will contend that research and evaluation are necessary tools of a ministry that desires to be accountable to Christ and his church. We cannot take communication effects for granted.[14]

In research, we often define effects in terms of cognitive belief, emotional affect, and behavioral intent. These can all be measured, and this may be all that is possible just after a certain "communication event," but we should not be satisfied unless we also measure long-term actual effects of cognitive improvements, affective changes, and behavioral steps.

We may, of course, be at the mercy of the effects we choose to observe. If our perspective is single-cause effects and causes, then we may be seriously diverted by the observed effects. For example, if we have a radio-ministry among a people where only young people write letters, but our "target audience" is the adult population, we may be totally misguided if we judge our results by letters received. It may cause us to produce programs for youth only in order to get letters.

It would seem helpful if effectiveness of Christian communication is defined from at least three perspectives: (1) the perspective of God, (2) the

---

14. James F. Engel, *How Can I Get Them to Listen*. Zondervan, 1977:13.

perspective of the Christian (the communicator), and (3) from the perspective of the receptor (the audience).

(1) For God, effectiveness will be seen from the *perspective of eternity*. God, as seen through his revelation, is concerned about *Shalom*, the presence of the kingdom of God. We find that all God's revelation and redemptive work is directed towards establishing this goal of harmonious relationships. God seems more concerned with obedience and faithfulness than with mere "evangelistic results."

(2) From the perspective of the *Christian communicator*, effectiveness will be seen in the light of *response* to the commission given by Christ: "go and make disciples of all nations" (Mt. 28:18–20). The commission also speaks of baptism and of incorporation into the life of the local congregation. It speaks of nurture and the instruction in all things pertaining to the kingdom of God. Since this is a comprehensive mandate and since the Lord has provided a variety of spiritual gifts to carry out this comprehensive ministry, it follows that no one person will participate in all its varied dimensions. Some will plant, others water, and yet others will harvest (1 Cor. 3:5–9).

(3) The effectiveness of Christian communication will from the perspective of the *receptor* be judged in relation to how he or she experiences *needs met*, and how a new joy and fullness of life in fellowship with God and with other human beings is experienced. As a result of God's intervention in his or her life, changes should be evident in such areas as values and self-esteem.

COMMUNICATION DEFINED

Communication is not something accidental and supplementary for human beings. We communicate because we, from our beginnings, are communicators by nature. The average person spends most of his or her active time communicating: listening, speaking, reading, writing, watching television and video. The interest in communication studies is also increasing, and almost every discipline concerned with human society and human behavior has during the last few years concerned itself with communication. A widening interest is also evident in Christian ministry.

The word communication has, like a number of other familiar words, developed from the Latin word *communis* which means to share, to have in common. Present day English derivatives still retain this concept of commonality.

Communication	*—sharing information and ideas*
Commune	*—living together on a property; sharing relationship*
Community	*—having geography or interests in common*
Communion	*—showing deep friendship, and also intimate sharing.*

These words point to relationships. It is thus impossible to separate the word communication from implications of mutual involvement and relationship, the development of commonality between people.[15] We can also notice that God seems to work primarily among and through communities.[16] Without constantly engaging in acts of communication with other human beings, none of us could develop the mental processes and social nature that distinguishes us from other forms of life, and without important communications systems, such as language, we could not carry out group activities or lead independent lives. Consequently, community should be demonstrated, both within Christian programs and among the people who produce the programs.[17]

Our communication messages must be designed as a process that corresponds to the needs of a receptor at his or her present position or stage in life, and the needs and problems faced at that time. A person's relationship with God can be seen as a spiritual journey and if we know a person's position in this journey, we can design communication events that will be relevant at this time.

Essentially, the communication process consists of information-processing organized around a shared orientation or topic.[18] Ordinarily this

---

15. Donald K. Smith, "Using Communications in the Kingdom of God." Study paper for Consultation on World Evangelization. Nairobi: Daystar Communications, 1979:5. See also, Donald K. Smith. *Creating Understanding*. Grand Rapids: Zondervan, 1992.

16. Charles J. Mellis, *Committed Communities, Fresh Streams for World Missions*. William Carey Library, 1976.

17. Francis A. Gray, *Radio in Mission*. Lausanne Committee for World Evangelization, 1989.

process is portrayed as occurring between poles designated as interpersonal and mass communication, but it can also take place within the thought processes of the individual.

THE MEDIA OF COMMUNICATION

Each individual media channel has its own possibilities and limitations and such possibilities change if it functions alone or in conjunction with other media. Discussion of the advantages and disadvantages of the various media, or the relative strengths of one method as compared to another, should therefore be carried on within a clear frame of reference.

Actually, to ask the question, "which medium is best?" is, not a very professional question, as it all depends on the situation.[19] The more relevant question is one of media mix, or rather, of using the right medium at the right time. Is it used according to the inherent and obvious advantages of that particular medium or method in that particular situation? A realistic view of a medium's capabilities will, therefore, need an intercultural analysis, and an appreciation of external factors influencing the use and application in a given context. Each society has ascribed roles to each medium, so it is helpful to work out a general list of advantages and disadvantages of the individual media channels.

It is easier to describe the media than to define media. In popular usage "The Media" refers to the whole complex of broadcasting, particularly television, and its many uses. In McLuhan terminology, media are extensions of the human body, and of the basic human communication symbols.[20] It is often helpful to see the media this way. The microphone becomes an extension of the voice, the pencil an extension of the hand, and the camera an extension of the eye. In Christian communication, we are channels through which the gospel of Jesus Christ is extended to others, and we use media to extend ourselves and our message to others.

---

18. Wilbur Schramm and Donald Roberts, *The Process and Effects of Mass Communication*. University of Illinois Press, Rev.Ed., 1971:22.
19. Andreas Fuglesang, *Applied Communications in Developing Countries*. Dag Hammarskjold Foundation, 1973.
20. Marshall McLuhan, *Understanding Media: The Extensions of Man*. McGraw-Hill, 1964.

To assure correct programming, we need to constantly engage in pre-testing of programs, as well as in other forms of research and evaluation. Most mistakes can be avoided by a regular use of evaluation and pretesting procedures.

THE USE OF COMMUNICATION MODELS

Due to the complexity of theories and classifications, it is helpful to utilize conceptual models when describing communication theory and media use. In a sense, this is like the apostle Paul describing the church as a body with many members, or the pastor including an illustration in the sermon.

Conceptual models are imaginative mental constructs invented to illustrate certain activities or situations. They are not literal pictures of the world, but illustrations used to develop or describe a theory which in some sense explains the situation.

The model is, therefore, an attempt at explaining how the mind of the model-constructor understands reality, and for most people, theories are easier to understand when explained on conceptual models. But as they are only pictures of reality as reality is understood at this time, they need to be dynamic in nature.[21] New knowledge may help us understand reality better, and consequently force the adaptation or change of models.

The actual process of communication is more complicated than any picture we are able to construct, and no one model is sufficient to explain and illustrate all aspects of the communication process. Some models will help us understand the process of communication, others will help us to understand how human beings interact and actually communicate with one another. Together they provide us with frames of reference within which we can discuss communication processes, variables and effects. Furthermore, models help us identify the elements in a communication process for analysis and study.

One topic that is of special interest for the media researcher is the concept of filtering. During the reception of a message, a selective filtering takes place in the mind of the listener. The filter can be illustrated in different ways, but it will include at least the following four stages: (1) *Exposure*: that is, a person is exposed to the message, listens to the radio when

21. Charles H. Kraft, *Christianity in Culture*. Maryknoll, NY: Orbis Books, 1979.

the program is on or when sitting in the pew during the sermon. (2) *Attention*: we must go beyond exposure. The attention must be there while listening to the sermon, and a person must pay attention to the radio, as well as the sign at the roadside. (3) *Comprehension*: it is important that the message is understood correctly so that information processing can take place. (4) *Retention*: a message must be remembered if action is to take place.

All of these stages in the filtering process are selective, that is, it is the receiver who controls the filter, deciding to open or close. An important aspect of communication research is, then, to discover how the filter operates. The central controlling factor is the evaluative criteria, in terms of which a person evaluates an incoming signal and influences the filter. The evaluative criteria is strongly influenced by a person's previous information and experience with the subject or person in question. If experience with the church is negative, a negative evaluative criterion will be the result, and this could have serious consequences for the messages communicated.

The field of communication research is still a new field. There is an enormous need for basic communication research that will help Christian communicators better understand their task and be more effective in communicating the message of Christ through media.

A COMPREHENSIVE MODEL OF THE COMMUNICATION PROCESS

The following development of a comprehensive model is a step-by-step approach to identifying the dimensions involved in effective communication.

In the comments provided for each step, several questions are raised. These are the questions we need to answer through our research activities.

1. Source/sender: The Communicator

In dealing with Christian communication, we have a message "to proclaim to the nations." Our primary concern is that all people everywhere may hear the gospel of Jesus Christ in ways that are relevant and understandable. So, we need to begin with ourselves, our purpose, our assumptions, and our limitations.

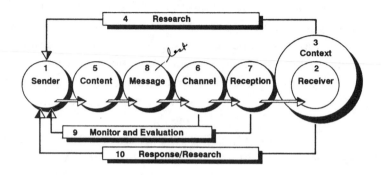

Figure 2. 1
Comprehensive Model of Communication Process

2. The Receiver: The Audience

Basic to effective communication is a good understanding of the audience. Who is the person or group we are trying to reach? What are the needs? Which topics are of interest? Are we dealing with young people or the older generation, Christian or non-Christian, educated or uneducated?

3. The Context of the Audience

It is not only a question of who is in the audience, but also where. Is my radio listener having breakfast, driving a car on a busy freeway, or watching buffaloes in a field? Is my reader among Christians, or is he or she in a hostile environment? Similarly, the context of the sender influences the way in which he or she communicates. There may also be serious limitations on media use.

4. Research: Getting the information

This is the activity needed to get the information mentioned in steps 2 and 3. Research can be both formal and informal, but our primary concern is to gain significant information about our audience so that our messages can be received in understandable terms. No one has earned the right to engage in media production without a clear understanding of the audience and their needs. We need to get such information before engaging in actual production. Good and appropriate research facilities are required to carefully analyze the needs of our audience.

5. Selection of Content

After defining the needs, we must come up with answers. As far as biblical content is concerned, a helpful approach to the selection of basic content for a program or a message is to follow these steps: (1) What is the general teaching in the Word of God about this need or topic? (2) Where do I find Bible passages that deal with this topic? (3) Which passages would be most helpful in meeting the needs of my audience? Then, it will indeed be "Good News To Needs."[22]

6. Identifying the Channel

Which communication approach or medium would be best suited for my communication with the chosen audience? How could I best communicate the selected content so that the needs of the receptors will be met? Would the situation call for a mass medium like television? Or, would an audio cassette be better? Maybe a church service should be utilized, or a visit by a friend. Each approach will give new dimensions and possibilities.

7. Reception

Here we are concerned with exposure to the message, captivating the attention of the audience, gaining understanding, and commitment to retention and action. During the reception of a message, numerous variables are at work, some hindering reception, some trying to block the communication. Define such variables as clearly as possible prior to the development of the program format. In other words, where is the receptor during the communication event, and which contextual factors will influence the reception?

8. Formulating the Message

The message or program format will depend on the media chosen. In a personal discussion, it will be words and body language. On radio it will be limited to sound in a combination of speech, music and sound effects. Film can use movement and visuals. Formulating the message is the task of translating ideas and thoughts into programs that can be communicated by a certain medium or approach in a format and style that will be of

---

22. For a practical guide to this, see: Viggo Søgaard, *Audio Scriptures Handbook*. United Bible Societies, 1991.

interest to the chosen audience. Which format and presentation will be most appropriate?

9. Monitoring and Evaluation

In secular communication, advertisers could not imagine spending huge sums of money on commercials without careful evaluation of programs and relevant monitoring of all aspects in the process, in particular the reception. Who listened to my program? Who read the tract? Did they understand my sermon? Are they taking action?

10. Response and Research

As Christian communicators we may seem to be satisfied with meager feedback obtained by mail. It is important to have such response through mail or telephone, but our response systems must be appropriate to all in the audience, including the non-literate. It is also important to have effective research designs that will measure the actual results. The most important question to ask is, Did we achieve our objectives and reach our goals?

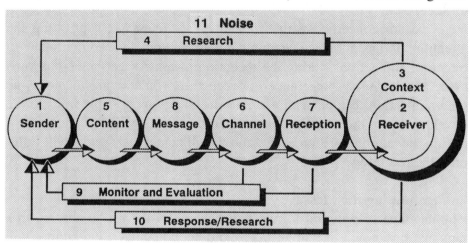

Figure 2. 2
Communication Process in Context of Noise

11. Noise

Noise is a technical term that describes anything that hinders good communication. Unfortunately, it affects all aspects of the communication process. Noise in the sender may give rise to biased programs, and noise in the receptor may change the meaning. Noise in the channel may give poor reception, and noise in the reception context may distract the listener or viewer. We must do all we can to reduce noise to an acceptable level so that the messages can come through as clearly as possible. Have potential noise factors been identified? Has corrective action been taken?

✱

FOUR KEY RESEARCH QUESTIONS FOR CHRISTIAN COMMUNICATION

1. *Who is my listener/reader/viewer?*
2. *Where is my listener/reader/viewer?* (car, church) needs?
3. *What are the needs of my listener/reader/viewer?*
4. *How can I meet the needs of my listener/reader/viewer?*

3

RESEARCH AND COMMUNICATION STRATEGY

In the previous chapter we discussed Christian communication theory and its relation to research. Such an approach is only possible, though, if there is a clear framework of a research-based strategy. In this chapter we will focus on two models that are selected because of the important contribution they can make to the development of research design. One is a strategy development model, and the other is a spiritual decision model. Both of them will demand good research.

STRATEGY AND CHRISTIAN COMMUNICATION

The term "strategy" was originally used as a military term and as such reminds some people of strategies of war. But for most, the term is merely a convenient word for describing any kind of plan. And, it is the conviction of this writer that strategy has deep roots in Scripture and that it is of central importance for Christian communication.

God seems to be working within a strategy framework. We can see strategy in the way he called Abraham, a specific person, so that he might bless all nations through him (Gen. 12:3; Gal. 3:8). He called a specific nation, Israel, at specific times for specific purposes (or you could say, he created Israel for specific purposes). He sent his Son at a specific time in history for a specific purpose (Eph. 1:9–10). Jesus, in turn, used a similar strategy, selecting a small and specific group of people (Mt. 3:13–19), training them and sending them out with a specific commission (Mt. 28:18–20). It was a strategy that was to begin in Jerusalem, then Judea and Samaria, and then the ends of the world (Acts 1:8). The Holy Spirit selected certain people at specific times for specific goals, such as Paul to go to the Gentiles (Acts 9:15). Paul was well prepared and equipped for this cross-cultural ministry, and he could approach people and work within frames of reference that were different from his own culture, attitudes, and religion (1 Cor. 9:19ff). Consider also this Old Testament illustration. Among the thousands of men who came to David at Hebron were the strategists from Issachar, "Of Issachar men who had understanding of the times, to know what Israel ought to do, two hundred chiefs" (1 Chron. 12:32). In other words, they were strategists who had a good information system. In the mission of the church today, we also need strategists who understand the times and can give guidance concerning what we need to do.

STRATEGY DEFINED

As a general definition of the term strategy, we can say that a strategy is an overall approach, plan, or way of describing how we will go about reaching our goal or solving our problem.[1] Strategy is a way to reach an objective, a kind of map of the territory to be covered in order to "reach from here to there."

Strategy is a conceptual way of anticipating the future, guiding us in major decisions concerning alternative approaches and decisive action. In this way strategy helps us by providing a sense of direction and cohesiveness, focusing on the central issues of our task and philosophy of ministry. It provides us with a frame of reference in which different aspects of theory can be seen in relationship and in their relative and interrelated application to the communication process.

We could also say that Christian communication strategy is the process of planning with an aim to align our plans with God's plans, seeking his

---

1. Edward R. Dayton and David A. Fraser, *Planning Strategies for World Evangelization*. MARC, 2nd Edition, 1990:13.

will for us and our ministry. Edward R. Dayton and David A. Fraser aptly call it a statement of faith:[2]

> *As Christians, a strategy forces us to seek the mind and will of God. Strategy is an attempt to anticipate the future God wants to bring about. It is a statement of faith as to what we believe that future to be and how we can go about bringing it into existence.*

The development of such a strategy will involve the study of Scriptures, prayer, and relying on the work of the Holy Spirit. But it is my conviction that it will also need data collection, research and analysis. This conviction is based on personal experience with communication research and on the significant amount of research experience gained by colleagues.

Strategy development demands goal-setting. As such, strategy makes it possible for us to measure effectiveness and helps us to visualize steps leading to the ultimate goals. A strategy, then, helps us develop effectiveness measurements, both for the ultimate goals as well as for intermediate goals.

Strategy development also includes decisions on media development or "media mix." This means that the theoretical framework leads to practical decisions concerning which media should be used, and when, and for what purpose a particular medium should be selected, or which kind of program is needed at a particular time or phase of the communication process.

Strategy based on a receptor-oriented communication theory is also needed to guide us in intercultural applications. A lack of such strategic understanding may otherwise leave us with canned approaches that in reality are merely the application of monocultural methods. A genuine attitude of dialogue and a high regard for the other person is required as we approach intercultural strategy development.

STRATEGY PLANNING MODEL

When applying strategic thinking to the work of churches and missions, it has been found extremely helpful to use a circular strategy development

---

2. Ibid., p. 14.

model. The model is slightly adapted from basic strategy models developed by other writers, in particular Dayton and Fraser.[3] For each step of the process, research needs are identified.

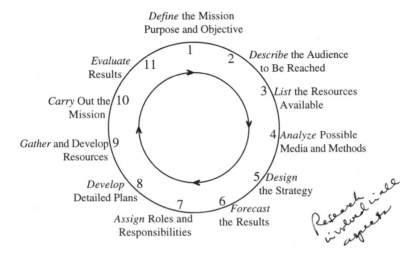

Figure 3. 1 Circular Planning Model

Step 1. Define the Mission Purpose and Objectives.

The first step in any planning process is to clearly define the purpose of the mission. Precisely what is it that we are trying to do? And why are we doing it? Our mission agency or church does not exist for our own sake but in order to fulfill certain specific purposes. If the purpose and objectives of our organization or church have been described in too broad terms, they are almost impossible to evaluate. A mission statement will need to include the mission distinctives and also be precise enough to guide in the development of the strategy and verify the results.

Research Helps Us Define the Mission. The work of the Holy Spirit is fundamental to all mission, and this cannot be planned or defined by research. On the other hand, we can through research document where the Spirit seems to be working. Visions are given by God, but mission is needed to translate vision into practical action. We often find pastors and other Christian leaders with great visions and with missions that have

---

3. Ibid.

been defined on the basis of experience and intuition. A research project can help to confirm if they are still on track, or otherwise help to redefine the mission at hand, and to explore new possibilities. Likewise, many media ministries can be helped by developing a clear definition of their mission or their target audience. Research can help to gather the information that will help them sharpen the vision and redefine the mission.

Many churches and organizations could profitably start by an analysis of what is actually happening because of their ministry. Such an analysis can describe the people being reached now, and with what results. It is important to know where we are.

Step 2. Describe the Audience to be Reached.

Who is my listener/reader/viewer? It will obviously make a difference in our planning if the person we are trying to communicate with is a new Christian, a church leader, or maybe a person from another religion with hardly any awareness of the Christian gospel at all. Does he or she have grave misunderstandings about the gospel? We must know as much as possible about our audience in order to reach them effectively. This calls for extensive research and constant involvement with the audience.

Research Helps Us Describe the Audience. Research can help us by providing a clear description of the audience and their needs. We need to study their relation to God and their understanding of the gospel. Such detailed information gathered prior to the start of a specific ministry will provide a basis for later evaluation of results.

A study of potential radio listeners may aim at describing the listening audience, their attitudes, interests and opinions, and then try to define them in terms of the spiritual decision model, which will be discussed later in this chapter. Listener needs and interests would then be able to direct the preparation of communication messages. Similarly, the study of a church may be conducted to obtain a clear description of its members for the purpose of developing a relevant teaching program.

Step 3. List the Resources Available.

Each mission will need resources. What is available for our present task? Who are the people we can draw on to help us? Where can we get financial resources? Who are the cooperating organizations that can assist us with necessary skills? Where can we get the necessary media products? It is important to be a "possibility thinker" and never limit our vision to the resources that are immediately available to us.

Research Helps Us Describe Our Resources. Through a thorough analysis we can list all the potential resources available for the task at hand. We often find that organizations that aim at reaching the same audience do not know the resources developed by the others and, consequently, there is an overlap and waste of resources. During a consultation in a certain Asian country, we discussed the needs of a specific, non-literate tribal group. Several missions were involved in reaching them, but we discovered, for example, that one group had produced a set of teaching cassettes several years earlier, but only a few copies had been distributed. The other organizations were not aware of their existence.

Step 4. Analyze Possible Media and Methods.

Here again, we need to think broadly. List all the possible media and methods that could be used to help us achieve our mission purpose among the chosen audience. Analyze each medium and approach for their advantages and disadvantages. Which approach would be most effective in this project?

In some countries, we have the luxury of being able to choose whatever medium we fancy, as they are available and free to be used by anyone with the necessary resources. In other countries, our choices may be very restricted due to the political situation. But in every case, we need to make intelligent choices, so that the most appropriate medium will be used.

Research Helps Us Analyze Media and Methods. Through experiments or pilot programs we can test approaches and gather information and experience as to the appropriateness of certain methods.

Marketing organizations will collect extensive data on the usefulness of individual media channels and their effectiveness in a given context, and we can obtain the results of such studies. Diffusion studies have, likewise, analyzed the effects of various methods, and how methods and media can be best integrated for reaching certain desired goals.[4] Some church growth studies have analyzed evangelistic campaigns and media ministries, but, generally speaking, there are very few studies on the com-

---

4. Everett M. Rogers, *Diffusion of Innovations*. The Free Press, 3rd Ed., 1983.

parative effectiveness and use of media from a Christian communication perspective. Often we need to do our own experiments.

Step 5. Design the Strategy.

At the fifth step in strategy development, we are making a sketch of what the actual strategy will look like. We will choose the media and the methods that should be used to reach our specific objectives, based on resources available. We will also make decisions on which media not to use. We cannot do everything, so a careful selection must take place.

Designing an approach may be more a selection process than actual research. It is the use of research data, case studies, and experimentation results that will guide us in developing realistic programs. Strategists do not need to be professional researchers, but they need to know how to interpret and use research data. Without the availability of research data, it would be extremely difficult to define an effective approach to Christian communication in a given country or context.

Step 6. Forecast Results.

Here we ask the tough question: If we follow this strategy, what can we realistically expect as results? If these are not satisfactory in relation to our objectives, we need to go back to step number one and work through the process once again in order to arrive at a strategy that we expect will give the desired results.

Research Helps Us Forecast Results. Dayton terms this point on the strategy planning model "Anticipated Outcome" which implies that we should, on the basis of research, be able to anticipate what the strategy can accomplish.[5] The forecasting of results can be helped by a comparison of results from similar projects, as well as from the results of pretesting and pilot programs.

Step 7. Assign Roles and Responsibilities.

This is a critical point if we are to see the strategy carried out. How much are we depending on ourselves and how much do we depend on others? A careful listing of roles and responsibilities will not only help us in

---

5. Edward R. Dayton and David A. Fraser, *Planning Strategies for World Evangelization*. MARC, 2nd Edition, 1990.

planning but will also safeguard us from running into serious complications in management and cooperation later on.

Step 8. Develop Detailed Plans.

This is the point where the "blueprint" is developed. As Jesus reminded us, we need to plan before building the house. We need to have the details put in order so that those involved in the mission can follow them. If many people are involved, a written plan can help to keep the focus on the real objectives.

Research Helps Us Develop Plans. During planning phases of a communications program, research can primarily help us by pretesting methods, programs, and other products. This could be testing an audio Scripture cassette, or it could be pretesting a magazine cover prior to publication. Such tests will give directions for future productions and distribution. Actual field testing can provide further insights before large sums of money are committed to expensive productions.

Step 9. Gather and Develop Resources.

Most likely the resources are not readily available. On the financial side, we may need to start a fund-raising drive. Tracts, radio programs, or films may have to be produced. Staff and volunteers may need to be trained. The primary purpose is to develop our resources so that they are ready for the mission to be carried out.

Step 10. Carry out the Mission.

Without this step the whole planning process will be futile. Here we put our faith and plans into action. Often this will demand great courage and faith on behalf of all involved. During this period good management will ensure that people, money, time, and programs are used in the right order and for the planned purposes.

All through the implementation phase, we need good monitoring systems. This could, for example, be a daily report on distribution or sales figures.

Step 11. Evaluate Results.

This final step is primarily one of research. Evaluation should be seen as an element of good stewardship. As the church entrusts resources to communication ministries, such ministries must be accountable for effective use of the resources. The primary question to ask is, Did we reach our objectives? If yes, what did we do right? If no, what did we do wrong? There is nothing wrong in failing as long as we learn from our mistakes!

Did we see results that correspond with the mission purpose and objectives? How can we learn from the results and redefine our objectives and redesign our strategy? What lessons have been learned that can assist us in becoming more effective in the future?

If we are evaluating the effects of media programs, we will also want to look at cost effectiveness of the media selection, and we will be asking specific questions such as, How many were actually exposed to the message, and what changes did the programs cause in their lives?

DEVELOPMENT OF A CONCEPTUAL STRATEGY MODEL

In the following, we will look at a comprehensive strategy model, also called a spiritual decision model. It is aimed at giving us an understanding of the audience and then providing a framework for the development of a comprehensive strategy. As such, it could be argued that the model should have been presented prior to the one above.

The Principles of a Total Program

The Great Commission (Mt. 28:18–20) calls us to preach the gospel to all people, make disciples from all nations, and then build up by Bible teaching. This gives us three general areas to which we can designate the more popular terms of sowing, reaping and refining. An early version of the model made this task visible.[6] This early version was a strictly cognitive model that on a biblical basis argued for a spiritual process rather than just an event.

This particular model has been used in studies to evaluate the effectiveness of specific ministries as well as to analyze target audiences. One of these research studies was an analysis of the listening audience to the

---

6. Viggo Søgaard, *Everything You Need to Know for a Cassette Ministry.* Bethany Fellowship Publishers, 1975:27.

Voice of Peace radio programs in Thailand.[7] The questionnaire was based on eighteen topics of biblical understanding, and the research data were then applied to the segmentation model. The result was a clear picture of the present position of the audience and their awareness of the gospel.

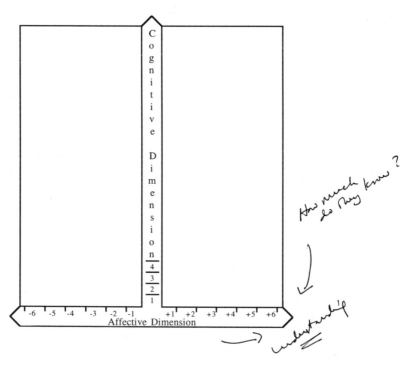

Figure 3. 2
Two-Dimensional Model with Both Cognitive
and Affective Dimensions

The model stimulated the design of similar models by other writers, and it can be found in several editions and forms as people have tried to adapt it to their particular situation or their way of thinking. The version developed by James F. Engel has become well-known around the world.[8]

---

7. Viggo Søgaard, "Radio Programming Research". Unpublished research report on radio listenership in Thailand, 1975.
8. James F. Engel, *How Can I Get Them to Listen*. Zondervan, 1977; and *Contemporary Christian Communication*. Thomas Nelson, 1979.

Engel has done much to coordinate the thinking and research of secular behavioral science with theological perspectives. To a large extent, he follows the paradigm of a linear approach to decision making: Knowledge-Belief-Attitude-Intention-Behavior, and he aptly applies the implications to the church and to the mission of the church.

A TWO-DIMENSIONAL STRATEGY AND DECISION MODEL

Based on the conviction that conversion is not an entirely cognitive process, the affective dimension has been added to make the model more useful. The affective dimension will primarily be a person's feelings towards the gospel, towards the church, and towards Christ. The actual decision is to a large extent an affective change, or change of allegiance. The result as seen in figure 3.2 is a matrix on which strategy can be developed. Through research we are able to discover a person's or a people group's position on the "chart."

Knowledge and Feelings

The vertical axis is the cognitive dimension. It is indicated as an ongoing process. There is no fixed conversion point, as a decision for Christ can theoretically take place at any stage of the cognitive process. Ideally, decisions should take place on the basis of a good cognitive foundation, but in practice we often see people becoming believers in Christ at a very low level of biblical knowledge. Such a situation will then demand heavy emphasis on cognitive input in the form of Bible teaching to safeguard and nurture further growth and permanent results.

At a recent research project among new believers in an Asian country, it was found that the affective and behavioral changes were much ahead of the cognitive changes.[9] Their feelings towards Jesus and their behavior in regards to prayer and Bible study was much ahead of their cognitive understanding of the gospel.

---

9. Confidential research report on Movement in Bangladesh. Submitted by Fuller Theological Seminary and Global Partners for Development, 1995.

Journey Towards Maturity

The journey towards spiritual maturity becomes a journey from one's present position towards "the upper right hand corner" of the model, as illustrated on figure 3.3. Most likely, this will not be a straight line as on this illustration, but it will fluctuate between cognitive and affective changes. Or both may take place at the same time. As already mentioned, conversion is to a large extent the crossing of the affective line from negative to positive, and it can occur at multiple places. Most lasting conversions will probably take place in the area indicated on figure 3.3. The line between negative and positive attitudes should possibly be broadened to allow for an area of non-commitment or neutrality. Each step in the spiritual decision process caused by our ministry can be seen as an evangelistic effect.

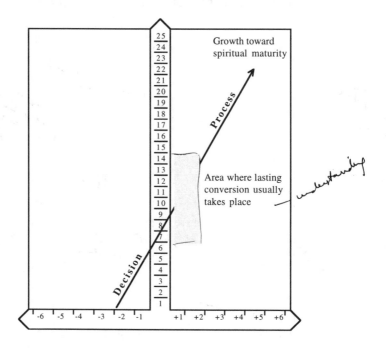

Figure 3. 3
Illustration of the Concept of Spiritual Progress

The development of a comprehensive, integrated strategy is like planning a "highway" from the present position of our audience to spiritual maturity. Each ministry or program becomes a section of the "highway" and must therefore be closely integrated. This will require clear sub-goals and strategies for each ministry involved. We cannot cause a person to walk on this highway, but we can make it possible.

Illustrations of Previous Journeys

In order to understand our audience, it is helpful to analyze an individual's or people group's movements up to this present time. In other words, we can map the "journey" which they have already taken. It is important for applied strategy (programming) to know where they have been, so that we can understand the knowledge and belief structures that form the basis for their present attitudes. Research can help us do exactly that.

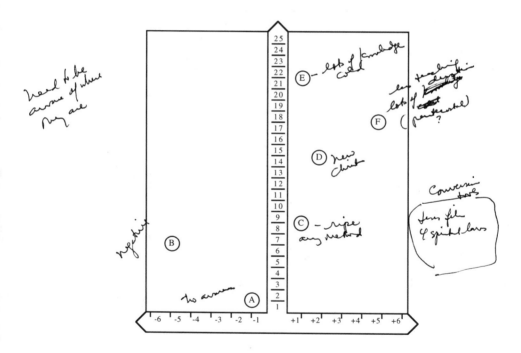

Figure 3. 4
Illustration of Various Audience Positions

Identifying the Position of our Audience(s)

The illustration in figure 3.4 shows six different potential audiences. On this example, "A" may be a tribal group with next to no awareness of the Christian gospel, but they are not really opposed or negative towards the gospel. "B" may be a group of young people in a Western country. They have been brought up in a Christian context, but they have been turned off by the church.

"C" is a field ripe for harvest. "D" is a new Christian, who has just accepted Christ as his or her Savior and Lord. "E" is a church which has been well taught in the Scriptures, but are pretty "cold" in their devotional life. "F" is a church which has had less teaching but excels in spiritual life and devotion.

Each of these audiences will need a different approach, and different strategies will need to be worked out to facilitate true spiritual growth.

Analyzing Our Present Reach

The model can also be used to illustrate the reach or areas of effectiveness of our present ministry, programs and evangelistic approaches. Much Western-produced evangelistic material is very limited in scope and does not reach much beyond the area of reaping. Development programs carried out by Christian agencies may cause significant changes in attitudes, but due to lack of integration, permanent spiritual results are lacking.

The emphasis by missions and local churches on the middle area of the model (conversion) is probably due to the lack of a comprehensive strategy, but it is also due to the limitations of our research measurements. Usually, our research has been too limited, so we have only measured conversions, baptisms or church membership. Such indicators relate to the middle section of our model. Consequently, our desire to measure effectiveness and show results has forced us to concentrate strategy development on areas that we have been able to measure. But any movement toward spiritual maturity should be seen as a measure of effectiveness, and research methodologies are available for measuring the movement.

Openness to Change

For any development of effective strategy and programs, we need to discover people's receptivity and openness to change. This can be done through careful research. At any position on the model, there will be a certain latitude of openness. The analysis of a group's position will not guarantee any changes or responses, but will help us to discover how to communicate with the person.

Some groups in a society are always more open to change than others, and at certain times in life we are more receptive to new ideas and to change than at other periods. We have to be extremely careful in our analysis, though. People may be closed to my approach rather than to the gospel, or my approach may actually be hindering a change.

By discovering the latitude of acceptance/rejection of our audience, we will also discover the extent of their openness to change. We may, for example, discover that some people may be open to the study of Scriptures as long as it is done outside a church building. Others will attend a social event at the church, but not a church service. Some will listen to a Christian radio program in the privacy of their own homes. The skillful communicator will use such insights in his strategy.

SUMMARY

Strategy planning is important to effective ministry, and there are helpful models that can serve as tools in the development of good and relevant strategies. The term strategy is a helpful term that describes an overall plan or approach as to how we are going to reach our objectives or solve our problems. It is a conceptual way of anticipating the future. As Christians, statements relating to our strategy objectives and goals are statements of faith. An eleven-step circular strategy development model was introduced as a useful tool that will help us ask the right questions and lead us through an orderly process of strategy development. Furthermore, it will guide us in planning relevant research designs.

We have also in this chapter presented a spiritual decision model. The purpose is to present a strategic framework for understanding the audience and develop strategies that relate directly to the spiritual process of the receivers. The model is built on two dimensions: knowledge and attitudes. It is not the intention that models should illustrate or answer all questions relating to spiritual decision processes, but to assist in strategy development.

We can conclude that refined research methodologies and techniques are available for Christian communication and when applied they will enhance the ministry and help us evaluate our effectiveness.

In summary, research for communication strategy can
- *sharpen the vision*
- *provide information on the audience*
- *make receptor-oriented communication possible*
- *help evaluate media products and programs*
- *assist in strategy development*
- *direct in goal-setting*
- *guide in planning*
- *test the effectiveness of ministry*
- *reveal the necessity of seeking the direction of God*

Section II

SURVEY RESEARCH

4

PURPOSE AND OBJECTIVES
OF RESEARCH

This chapter will deal with the first steps in a Survey Research Process. It will discuss the reasons for doing research. Secondly, the chapter will deal with development of a Research Purpose Statement and Research Objectives. Thirdly, there will be a treatment of other Preliminary Activities needed to prepare a successful research project.

REASONS FOR DOING RESEARCH: DEFINING THE PROBLEM

A research project requires detailed planning, and that includes a careful consideration of the need for the study before a decision to undertake research is taken. We have seen earlier that both management and research should be involved in this process, which in itself will signify a commitment by management to undertake the study and later phase the results into strategic applications.

But why should we engage in research? What is the nature of the problem that needs to be solved? We could start with the negative, that is suggesting a few wrong reasons for doing research. (1) A pastor or Christian leader may accept a research project to avoid criticism for not doing it. If the board of a church or mission organization has members who in their daily work use research as a way of making decisions, then they will want

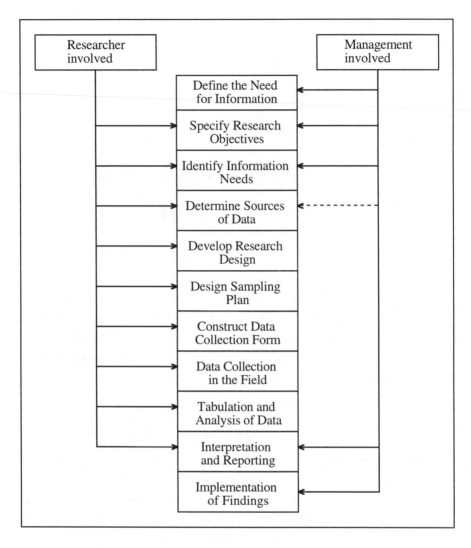

Figure 4. 1
Steps in the Survey Research Process

the same approach in the church. The pastor or leader may find it uncomfortable, but to avoid criticism, they commission some research. (2) Another wrong reason could be that a person wants to prove that he or she is right. If someone has been following the same approach for years, it is difficult to change, so research is seen as a way to justify the approach being followed. There will then be a big temptation to bias the research in that direction.

On the positive side, we need information that will help us make the right decisions. Many of us have often thought, *I wish I knew . . . I wish I knew how people in this community think about our church. I wish I knew who actually listens to my program so that I can make my program's relevant to them.* Research will, then, help us reduce error in the management decision-making process by providing insights into a certain situation.

In chapter one we discussed this decision-making process to which our research project must relate. From the management perspective, it is a process of *realizing the need for a decision, defining the decision problem, identifying possible solutions, evaluating alternatives, selecting an approach, implementation, and action.*

Following are examples of reasons that were established for some of the research projects referred to in this book.

A Media Advisor for the United Bible Societies is concerned about Bible communication with non-literate people. He is struggling with the issue of language and translation. In his research he wants to find out if there is a difference in the way literates and non-literates understand language. If there is a difference, then we need new Bible translations for reading the Scriptures on audio cassettes.[1]

A mission among a Muslim people in an Asian country was reporting thousands of new believers. There was apparently a people movement towards Christ, but the question was, Are these people real believers? Or, what do they believe? How many are there? How can a proper teaching plan be developed and what should be the content of such teaching?[2]

Several years ago, a Christian radio studio in Thailand needed a clear picture of their audience. How many listened? Who were they? Letter response was minimal, but it was also clear from other

---

1. Ph.D. Research by Julian Sundersingh from Fuller Seminary School of World Mission, Pasadena, California, 1996.
2. Confidential report on Movement in Bangladesh. Submitted by Fuller Theological Seminary and Global Partners Development, 1995.

research that the target audience was one that did not write letters. In order to prepare appropriate radio programs, producers needed reliable information about the audience, their interests, their background, and their felt needs. Such information could only be obtained through survey research.[3]

Another reason for doing research could be a church leader who wants to test the level of satisfaction with the church's program among its members. The results will be used by the church board in planning next year's program and activities.

Another church may want to survey the neighborhood around the church to plan a new outreach to the local community.

In summary, the following preliminary questions need to guide the thinking regarding a new research project.

1. *What do I need to know? (To make the right decision).*
2. *Why do I need to know this?*
3. *Where can I get the information?*
4. *From whom do I need the information?*
5. *When do I need it?*
6. *How will I use the information?*
7. *What will be the result of using this information?*

INTERRELATIONSHIP OF ELEMENTS IN THE RESEARCH PROCESS

In a research project, especially if it is a large one, it is important to keep a clear perspective and at all times be able to relate a specific activity to the process. Figure 4.1 provides a model for the whole research process, but the interrelationship of the various elements can be further illustrated as shown in figure 4.2.

In this perspective, each step flows into the next. A defined decision problem will guide in the development of research objectives. Research objectives will then require a certain identified set of information needs.

---

3. Viggo Søgaard, "Radio Programming Research." Unpublished research report on radio listenership in Thailand, 1975.

Information needs are translated into a questionnaire that will gather the necessary information from the study population.

The process is then reversed. The answers from the respondents are recorded on the form. Data from the field work will be tabulated and presented to answer the information needs. The results will be interpreted in relation to research objectives, so that management will be able to phase the knowledge into applied strategy that will aim at solving the decision problem at hand.

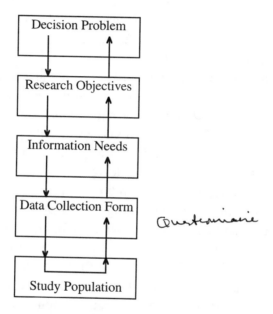

Figure 4. 2
Interrelationship of Decision Problem, Research Objectives,
Information Needs, Questionnaire, and Field Work

BASIC CRITERIA FOR A SUCCESSFUL RESEARCH PROJECT

A successful research project is a project that has been well prepared and carried out faithfully, and the results have been phased into applied strategy. In order to achieve this, we follow the principles of survey research, but there are also a few other basic criteria for a successful research project that need to be discussed.

Commitment by Management

The issue of management involvement in a research project is of utmost importance if the project is to have a successful conclusion. The pastor or leader who will be responsible for applying the results of the study will need to have a felt ownership of the study and a willingness to adhere to its findings. When a study is commissioned by board members or another person/group without the heartfelt consensus or support of the leader, then application of the final research report may be avoided. The results may cut across the opinions of the leader, and he or she may be tempted to find excuses for not putting the results into effect. Most researchers will have experienced such situations.

By having the leader involved in the early stages of the project, he or she can assist with information about the history of the church or the movement and as such can provide valuable information regarding information needs. They will also know the daily problems and situations that can provide qualitative information which will be important for development of appropriate research design.

As illustrated on the research process model in figure 4.1, management needs to be involved in defining the *Purpose for the Study* and in specifying the *Research Objectives*. This will be a joint activity between the leader and the researcher. The researcher will also discuss and identify *Information Needs* together with the leader/manager. The insights of the manager may also be important for identifying data sources.

But the actual research design, sampling procedures, and the whole area of data collection will be the task of the researcher in order to keep it as objective as possible. We do not expect that a pastor or leader can be totally objective in the data gathering process. There will always be the temptation to look for data that will make us look good.

When tabulation has been done, the manager is again brought into the process to help interpret the data so that appropriate reports can be prepared by the researcher. The researcher may provide suggestions for application and strategy, but it is the leader who decides on actual strategy implications and action steps.

If such a close relationship exists between the manager and the researcher, good research will be the result. On the other hand, if roles are not clearly understood, the results may be poor research and biased results.

Correct Questions Asked

In a successful research project, careful attention will be given to the selection of questions. The next chapter will deal with this issue as we discuss *Information Needs* to which questions on a questionnaire must relate. By carefully defining information needs, unnecessary work and the collection of useless data can be avoided. There will always be the temptation to satisfy one's own curiosity and ask questions that are not needed, but this can be avoided by careful work on information needs.

The concept of validity will also be treated later. For a research project to provide valid information, the information gathered must be the kind of information needed by the organization to solve their stated problems. Valid information is of high value, while invalid information is waste of resources.

To assure validity of information, careful attention will therefore need to be given to the initial stages in the research project: problem definition, purpose statement, development of objectives, and identification of information needs.

Appropriate Research Techniques Used

Closely related to the topic of Validity is the concept of Reliability. Reliability deals with the trustworthiness of the obtained data. The question we often need to ask ourselves is, *Are we measuring what we believe we are measuring?* Careful definition of terms will be necessary to give a positive answer to this question. Often we will be dealing with attitudes, opinions, and issues that are not directly observable, so we have to infer the answers from observable and measurable items. If constructs are not carefully defined, we may be seriously misguided in interpreting the data.

It is therefore important for a successful research project that careful attention is given to the development of an appropriate research design. Furthermore, when it comes to tabulation, the researcher will need to know and understand the type of data obtained and which statistical formulas can be used for that kind of data.

Findings Communicated Clearly

Towards the end of this section, we will be dealing with the *Research Report*. It is important to have a well-prepared report, but even more important to communicate the findings to the right people. If prior commitment from management has been obtained, there is a good chance for success.

But researchers are often tempted to show their professional knowledge by writing reports that are difficult to understand, and consequently do not communicate. This should be avoided. A written report in itself is normally not enough. The report has to be presented and the implications clearly communicated to those involved in using the data.

In a study regarding the communication of research reports, carried out by this writer, it was found that where the research report had only been communicated through print, that is, the printed report was presented to the pastor and the church board, then very little happened. The report was given a prominent place on the bookshelf. In other churches, where the researcher had been able to present the findings through an oral presentation to the board, or even better to the whole church, then the findings were usually followed.

Unfortunately, the lack of management involvement in research design, and the lack of clear communication of research findings have often resulted in unused research reports.

| Define the Need for Information |
| Specify Research Objectives |
| Identify Information Needs |

PURPOSE STATEMENT

When the decision has been reached to commission a research project in order to solve a decision problem, we then need to define the purpose of the research itself, preferably in one sentence. The purpose statement will be further defined by a set of specific objectives that will guide in the development of the research design.

A purpose statement will spell out what the research is all about, why it is being done, and what will be the intended result. If it can be action oriented, then it will be easier to relate it directly to the decision problem. A purpose statement is the guiding banner for the development of objectives and research design. Briefly stated, a research statement can be developed by filling out the blanks in the following sentence,

The purpose of this research project is to study_____ so that _____ will be able to _____

A few examples of research purpose statements would be:

The purpose of this research project is to have a close look at the present as well as potential audience of VOP in order to be as effective as possible in programming, and be able to integrate the ministry in a meaningful and comprehensive strategy together with churches and other media ministries.[4]

The purpose of this research is to study ministry approaches to Muslim ministries by selected churches and movements in [country] in order to (a) evaluate their extent and effectiveness, (b) discover underlying mission principles and contextual dynamics, and (c) develop a taxonomy of lessons that can guide in the selection of suitable approaches to other Muslim related people.[5]

The purpose of this research project is to conduct a product test on (a new translation of) Mark's Gospel (in Thai language) in order to determine its potential market in terms of responsive audience segments, and to gather data for a meaningful marketing strategy.[6]

---

4. Viggo Søgaard, "Radio Programming Research." Unpublished research report on radio listenership in Thailand, 1975.
5. Confidential report on Movement in Bangladesh. Submitted by Fuller Theological Seminary and Global Partners Development, 1995.
6. Viggo B. Søgaard, "Product Testing of Living Gospel of Mark in Thai." Unpublished research report, 1976.

The purpose of this study is to develop a theoretical framework for relevant use of radio and cassette media in the communication of the Gospel among Mainland Chinese.[7]

RESEARCH OBJECTIVES

After the development of a purpose statement, we need to define the actual parameters of the study through some specific objectives. Research objectives will be written down and presented to the management or leadership of the organization for acceptance prior to further development of the research design. It will be on the basis of such objectives that the data will eventually be interpreted and applied.

Taking the second examples given above, the objectives regarding a study of movements towards Christ were stated as follows:

Objective 1: To obtain demographic data about the extent of the movement in order to determine the number of believers.

Objective 2: To obtain information about the actual content of the faith professed in terms of cognitive, affective, and behavioral dimensions to determine extent of spiritual change.

Objective 3: To ascertain the methods by which the movement spread, how people were discipled, and how leaders were trained in order to discover basic missiological principles used in the movement and to understand underlying contextual dynamics.

For the radio research mentioned above in example one, the objectives were defined as follows:

Objective 1: To study radio listening habits, station and program preference by the audience.

Objective 2: To determine the size of present listenership.

Objective 3: To determine effectiveness of individual radio program series.

---

7. Research proposal for doctoral work at Fuller Seminary School of World Mission, Pasadena, California, by Helen Lim, 1995.

Objective 4: To gather demographic data on present audience.

Objective 5: To obtain value ratings by the target audience.

Objective 6: To do a spiritual segmentation and understanding study of the target audience by comparing listeners to non-listeners.

The objectives could also be stated as a series of research questions. For example four above, the research questions were stated as follows:

Research Question 1: What are the factors that significantly affect the effective use of radio and cassette in Christian ministry?

Research Question 2: What are the major cultural themes of the Mainland Chinese that should be taken into consideration when using radio and cassette media?

Research Question 3: How should the cassette and radio be programmed to meet the spiritual needs of the target audience in a relevant format?

Research Question 4: What factors will need to be considered for developing integrated media in ministry to Mainland Chinese?

INFORMATION NEEDS

Following the development of *Research Objectives*, we need to identify the information that will help us meet the objectives. As this is such an important stage in the research process, it will be treated in detail in the next chapter.

MORE PRELIMINARY ACTIVITIES

There are a number of other preliminary activities or steps that will further help make the research project good and useful.

Simulate the Results

It is often helpful to simulate the results, that is, try to visualize the whole research process, its individual steps, and the final results. This can be done prior to developing research design, but it is also an activity that can be carried out at other steps in the research process. It is a way of anticipating what will happen at each step and what problems may occur. It will also help us identify possible information needs that have been overlooked, and we can then make necessary adjustments prior to the actual study itself.

Visualizing the results will also help us decide on necessary cross-tabulations of data. This in turn will help select the appropriate demographic items that will be needed for making cross-tabulations. All through this exercise, we will be asking "What if . . . What then . . ." questions.

Develop Decision Criteria

At an early stage in the research process, it is helpful to decide on the decision criteria. The development of decision criteria is the process of establishing the rules for application of the data prior to the collection of data. If the establishment of decision criteria is not done before the research, or even more important before the management sees the actual results, there may be organizational priorities or biases that will influence the interpretation of the data. The establishment of rules regarding the use of data prior to field research will also safeguard a balanced use of experience and "old data" with the new data. If the rules are not present, we may assign too much weight to certain pieces of data.

Decision criteria can be stated in a number of ways. It can be a percentage, like "If 15% of the church members will answer positively to this question about a new publication, then . . ."

Often research will confirm present knowledge, and there may be the feeling that this is "nothing new." This in itself is valuable information, though, as it confirms and give a sense of certainty. Research can confirm that we are on the right course, or it can call us to change course.

Consider Cost vs. Benefits

The benefits of the results and the cost involved in obtaining the data need to be evaluated at all times. Cost is also associated with the type of research called for and not just if research should be carried out. This will again depend on the accuracy of the data needed. If only some preliminary information is needed, then it may be a waste of resources to conduct a full-scale probability sampling and survey research. If it costs 10,000 dollars to get a 500-dollar saving, only a fool would commission such research.

In much of the research needed by a church or mission organization, it is difficult to quantify benefits. The research may be exploratory for developing a new program, and benefits will then be judged in the light of felt benefits on behalf of the decision makers. The implied benefits may be very important for the future of the ministry, and in the long run benefits may be seen as both time and funds.

Develop Research Proposal

Several people are usually involved in a research project, so it is important to write a clear research proposal. The proposal is needed to get commitment to the whole project ahead of time. If funding will be needed from a foundation, then a detailed research proposal will need to be made. Also, if an outside research agency is involved, it is important to have the process and agreement clearly spelled out.

A study proposal will normally include a brief description of the background to the study, including the decision problem that calls for information.

The rationale for the study will be summarized in a purpose statement. Specific objectives needed to fulfill the purpose will then be outlined. It is also helpful if the proposal includes a list of information needs and a description of data sources.

The proposal will also include a timeline and cost analysis. For a proposal aimed at obtaining financial support for a project, there will need to be a description of the people and organizations involved and their background skills in the area of research and mission.

5

INFORMATION NEEDS
AND DATA SOURCES

Specify Research Objectives
Identify Information Needs
Determine Sources of Data
Develop Research Design

The constant question in the mind of the researcher and the decision maker will be, "*what do I need to know in order to answer the question at hand?*" There are many things which may be of interest, but the question is not what I would like to know, but what I *need* to know. A list of specific information needs will be developed prior to proceeding with research design, sample definition, and questionnaire construction.

RESEARCH OBJECTIVES AND INFORMATION NEEDS

If research objectives are given in great detail, they may seem to overlap with information needs. In turn, detailed information needs may seem to overlap with questions on the questionnaire. But it is important not to be misguided by such perceptions. The exercise involved in developing information needs has proved to be of great value in research design.

Research objectives identify the areas in which we need information. Information needs specify the information we need to have to meet the objectives, and questions on the questionnaire are formulated in such a way that they will obtain that information.

The list of information needs then forms the link or bridge between the research objectives and the questionnaire. In turn, the questionnaire will form the link between the information needs and the data to be collected.

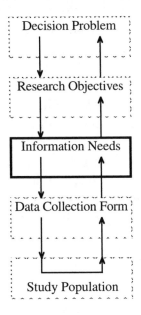

Figure 5. 1
Function of Information Needs in Research Process

DEFINING NEEDED INFORMATION

The identification and selection of information needs is the process of identifying the data that can fulfill the objectives. The process will, at the same time, screen out data that we do not need.

Let us take an illustration from the field of medicine. If a person is not feeling well, he or she will go to a medical clinic or hospital. The doctor attending to the patient will have available numerous possible tests: blood tests, x-rays, listening to the heart, temperature, blood pressure, etc. For his or her "research," the doctor will only select a few tests and on the basis of information obtained form these tests, a diagnosis will be made and the necessary treatment prescribed.

Similarly, in communication research we do not try to use all possible tests or get all possible information. A selection will need to take place. Often we will begin with a long list of information needs which will then be reduced through careful weighing of the alternatives. The study will need to be manageable in size and within reasonable cost. By beginning with a long list we have a greater chance of selecting the most important information needs than if we just started with a very short list.

For the research of a people movement's journey towards Christ, which was referred to in the previous chapter, a careful listing of topics was developed. In order to judge the level of Bible knowledge and general spiritual position, numerous areas could be studied, but in consultation with experts, it was decided to focus information gathering on four categories and for each category to look at three dimensions.[1] The categories were Jesus (God), Salvation (forgiveness), Church (the people of God), and the Scriptures. For each topic, the study would focus on cognitive (knowledge), affective (feelings), and behavioral (doing) dimensions. It was believed that on the basis of such information it would be possible to describe the movement and its results, and then develop appropriate teaching strategies. Stated differently, the information needs were identified as follows:

- *What do they know about Jesus?*
- *How do they feel towards Jesus?*
- *How do they act in relation to Jesus?*

- *What do they know about salvation?*
- *How do they feel regarding salvation (forgiveness)?*
- *How do they act regarding salvation?*

---

1. Research carried out in Bangladesh, Nigeria, and Ethiopia under the auspices of Fuller Seminary School of World Mission, 1995–96.

- *What do they understand about the church (people of God)?*
- *How do they feel towards other believers?*
- *How do they behave in relation to other believers?*

- *How do they understand the Scriptures?*
- *What are their feelings regarding the Scriptures?*
- *How do they use the Scriptures?*

Obviously, many other topics could have been selected, but those who were knowledgeable about the situation found the selection acceptable. From the above illustration it can also be seen that information needs are questions we have and not questions to go on the questionnaire. For this particular study we needed to develop questions with an appropriate format so that they could provide us with process measures. That is, for each of the information needs listed above, a measuring instrument needed to be developed.

If our research objective had been to make a demographic study of a congregation, our information needs would have dealt with issues like age, gender, education, income, family, and occupation. All issues that would help us describe the members in a certain church.

INFORMATION NEEDS WILL ASSURE THE PROVISION OF INFORMATION AND NOT JUST DATA

Data can be very interesting, but if the collected data cannot be directly translated into information that will help solve our problem, it may be useless. A well-developed list of information needs will assure that the data collected is useful.

It is helpful to conceptualize the information-gathering process, or try to visualize the situation. We need to ask ourselves questions such as:

- *Can I get the information?*
- *Can I get it from the right people?*
- *If I get it, what will I actually learn from it?*
- *Can I be sure that the data will give me the information I expect it to give?*
- *How will I be able to use this information?*
- *Will the availability of this information actually help me solve the problem at hand?*

Research Purpose	Questions designed to obtain the information
Research Objective #1	
Information Need 1.1	Questions number
Information Need 1.2	Questions number
Information Need 1.3	Questions number
Information Need 1.4	Questions number
Information Need 1.5	Questions number
Research Objective #2	
Information Need 2.1	Questions number
Information Need 2.2	Questions number
Information Need 2.3	Questions number
Information Need 2.4	Questions number
Information Need 2.5	Questions number
Research Objective #3	
Information Need 3.1	Questions number
Information Need 3.2	Questions number
Information Need 3.3	Questions number
Information Need 3.4	Questions number
Information Need 3.5	Questions number
Information Need 3.6	Questions number

Figure 5. 2
Form for Checking Relationship of Purpose,
Objectives, Information Needs and Actual Questions

reliability + validity   *Question that answer the objectives - in different parts*

RELATIONSHIP BETWEEN PURPOSE, OBJECTIVES, INFORMATION NEEDS, AND QUESTIONNAIRE

The form presented in figure 5.2 can be used as an overview of the relationship and the process. Just fill in the actual statements and questions. The filled-out form will be needed when we get to data interpretation and reporting towards the end of the study.

involves Communication arts Creativity etc.

In summary, the same way as the objectives are directly derived from the purpose statement, and the information needs are based on the research objectives, so there needs to be a direct correspondence between the information needs and questions on the questionnaire. Often several questions will be needed to answer one information need, and at other times, the same question will relate to several different information needs.

CASE STUDY: EXAMPLE OF RESEARCH PROJECT WHERE INFORMATION NEEDS WERE CAREFULLY DEVELOPED

Church Diagnostic Research

This particular study is exploratory and descriptive in nature, trying to define potential or actual audiences and to gain information about spiritual position, depth of Bible understanding, needs and interests. The purpose is to aid management in decision-making concerning strategy, media selection and programming content.[2]

Background Information

A Christian organization had for many years been working in difficult countries with authoritarian governments. One main activity had been Bible distribution to Christians in the so-called closed countries. The organization had also tried to assist churches and individual Christians in such countries. In the course of this ministry they had seen some strong Christian groups survive even the most difficult adversity and persecution, yet they had also seen that most churches were not prepared or equipped to face such difficult times and survive.

As the organization looked at the world and the political situation in various countries it became evident that some countries would, most likely, soon be under authoritarian governments which were far from positively inclined towards the Christian church. Leaders of the organization

---

2. Viggo B. Søgaard, "Church Research Study." Unpublished report on the status of several denominations in Thailand, 1978.

began to wonder how the churches would be able to face persecution, and, how could a church be prepared before the winds of political change would come? It is easier to help a church while freedom exists than when prohibitions rule.

The main research question was, How can we prepare a church to live and survive under a hostile, authoritarian government?

Preliminary Study

In order to set guidelines and parameters for the research project we needed mutually acceptable objectives. To achieve that, various preliminary studies were made. We needed to understand:

- *The situation of a persecuted church.*
- *The kind of church that survives.*
- *The situation of the present church.*
- *The needs of the present church.*
- *The strategy needed to prepare the church.*

The first step was to study books, articles and unpublished material concerning the situation in countries such as China after the Maoist revolution. Interviews were conducted with people who had lived through such times and been subjected to brainwashing attempts. Numerous meetings with Christian leaders and teachers took place. An ongoing study group was organized and a special nine-week unobtrusive study of nine churches in North Thailand was conducted. Data from other research studies conducted in Thailand was consulted and analyzed. This provided information on the context of the churches in Thailand, which were to be used as our test-area. Different studies on media were available, indicating channels of effective communication in that country.

Objectives

Finally, the following specific objectives were set for the research project:

- *To define the kind of church that would be successful under hostile, authoritarian rule.*
- *To measure the church in Thailand as to how it reflects that picture.*
- *To uncover possible avenues of communication.*
- *To suggest what should be done while open evangelism is possible in the country.*
- *To have a pretested model for church diagnostic tests.*

Each of these objectives almost becomes a purpose statement in itself due to the complexity of the study. We could summarize these points and say that the overall purpose was to plan a research-based communication strategy that would aim at equipping a church to function in a hostile environment.

Definitions

In order to carry out measurements we needed to define terms and measurement scales. What was the true, real, ideal apostolic church like? What would the "successful" church living under authoritarian rule be like? Somehow, the research project needed that ideal as a measuring standard.

After further study and correspondence, the following eight points were agreed upon as being the points we needed to measure. We could call these objectives for the sub-purpose of *defining a church that would be successful under hostile, authoritarian rule.* Other points or categories could possibly have been selected, but we found these to be most important:

1. *A church that knows the power of the Holy Spirit in their daily lives.*
2. *A church that experiences the fellowship of the body of Christ.*
3. *A church that knows the Bible.*
4. *A church that is serious about evangelism.*
5. *A church that is committed to serve the needs of society.*
6. *A church that is self-supporting and free from outside power and control.*

7. *A church that knows the strength and weaknesses of those who oppose the church.*

8. *A church that is brave and ready to witness in the face of persecution.*

A fairly long definition was then given for each point. This was needed for the purpose of working out and defining the measuring scales. Following is a translation of two of these original definitions or explanations:

• A church that knows the Bible (objective 3)

This is a church that reads the Bible, teaches and preaches from the Bible. They learn the truth of God from the Bible through faith and the inspiration of the Holy Spirit. They memorize Scripture as a preparation for witnessing. It is a church that follows the teaching of the Bible and resists false teaching.

• A church that is self-supporting and free from outside power and control (objective 6)

A church that understands what it means to be Christian and are prepared to serve God. It understands the responsibilities of the church to be self-supporting, not relying on help from other places. It is a church that equips their own leaders, letting them receive training so that they will be able to lead well. They teach the responsibilities all Christians have to help each other, and they give their offerings without expecting anything in return. It is a church that relies directly on God in all things.

These two definitions are given as illustration, but they clearly show us that we are dealing with issues that are all very difficult to measure, and many of the points cannot be tested directly. Results have to be inferred from direct questioning and observation. For this purpose we needed to clearly define our information needs.

Information Needs

Arriving at a list of information needs was difficult because of the topics involved and there were no other previous studies to learn from. It was

To define the kind of church that would be successful under hostile, authoritarian rule.	Questions designed to obtain the information
Objective 1: A church that knows the power of the Holy Spirit in their daily lives.	
1. Have they been converted?	1, 2, 23, 24, 44
2. Have their lives been changed?	25, 43, 44
3. Are they showing a humble life?	26, 43, 44
4. Do they have daily experience with the Holy Spirit in their lives?	13, 14
5. Do their lives show love?	14, 44
6. Do they receive teaching in their lives through the Holy Spirit?	25, 33, 48
7. Do they trust in God's power?	39, 40, 44
8. How is their prayer life?	38, 44, 50
Objective 2: A church that experiences the fellowship of the body of Christ.	
1. How is their worship and other religious ceremonies?	12 (and 2nd questionnaire)
2. How does their fellowship show?	15, 41
3. What gifts of the Spirit do they have and how do they serve the church?	13
4. What is their form of fellowship?	33
5. What help do they feel they receive from fellowship with one another?	32, 33, 41
6. How close is the fellowship between them?	15, 34
Objective 3: A church that knows the Bible.	
1. How do they read their Bibles?	3, 4
2. How is the studying and teaching of the Bible, both personally and in the church?	5, 7, 20, 33, 34, 36
3. What is their Bible knowledge?	24, 27, 28, 30, 45–49
4. How much faith do they have in the Word of God?	27, 28, 29, 41, 42
5. How many Bible verses do they memorize?	6, 31, 44–49
6. How is the Bible used in preaching?	6, 31, 45–49
7. Do they use the Bible in their testimony as well as in solving life's problems?	45–49
8. Are they able to use the Bible to refuse false teaching?	31, 38, 45–49
9. Do they have Bible reading and worship in their families?	7

Figure 5. 3
Illustration of Information Needs and Corresp. Questions

important to define the types of information needed in order to meet the specific requirements of the objectives. For each of the eight headings, a list of information needs was constructed. If we gained information on these points it was believed that we would be able to answer the objectives of the research project. An illustration is provided in figure 5.3.

The illustration shows the defined information needs for the first three points. For each information need there is a reference to the relevant questions on the questionnaire. We can see that for some needs there are several questions, and on the other hand, the same questions will often provide information on a number of different issues.

Design

The field research was conducted in eight different areas, covering five different denominations. In each denomination or district, churches were selected randomly. The actual method used differed, but it was primarily a case of drawing lots. The method used for data collection was self-administered questionnaires in group interviews. In this way we were sure of 100% response, and immediate answers could be provided to respondent's questions concerning methodology. At the same time, the anonymity of the individual respondent was safeguarded.

During, or just after a church service a group of members were randomly selected from those present in church that day. Each one chosen was asked to remain after the service to help fill out a questionnaire.

The responsibility for field work was given to one assistant, and in most cases he was present during the sessions when questionnaires were filled out. A group of pastors and missionaries were given instructions and supervised the field work in their specific areas.

The Questionnaire

The construction of the questionnaire was a formidable task. It had to be self-administered and it used a variety of scales and types of measurement. It was a fairly long questionnaire, which a highly literate person could fill out in 20–30 minutes (as done during pretesting), and up to two hours for those who were just functionally literate.

In order to gain a good acceptance and willingness to respond, the following introduction (translated from Thai) was given on the questionnaire:

- *This questionnaire is not an examination, but we need to have your exact answers to the questions in order to see how they apply to your life at this time.*
- *The purpose of this survey is to get information about Christians in Thailand in the areas of faith, society and life. The results will be used to change and improve the work of the church. You do not need to put your name on the questionnaire because we do not need to know your name. We only need to know your answers.*
- *We realize that considerable time is needed to answer the questions, but please do help us to finish it for the sake of the Lord's work in the future. Thank you very much.*

As mentioned earlier, some of the information needs required several questions. The use of multiple questions on the same issue also served to check the accuracy of information gained and to understand the true meaning of the responses.

As an example, let us look at objective 3, information need 5 which was designed to test how many Bible verses they remembered by heart. Eight different questions were used:

Question 6 was a direct, undisguised question:
   "How many Bible verses do you know by heart?"

Question 31 was designed to find out if the respondent could identify John 14:6:
   "If someone says, there is no real truth, how will you answer?"
   (a) No answer.
   (b) Agree with him.
   (c) Don't know how to answer.
   (d) Quote John 14:6.
   (e) Quote Luke 1:1.
   (f) Quote Romans 12:8.
   (g) ....

Question 44 was part of a series of AIO (Attitudes, Interests and Opinions) sentences to which the respondent was asked to indicate how much he or she identified with the sentence. One sentence said,

> *"I can remember Bible verses, but I cannot remember the references."*

There were four levels of answers possible.

Question 45 was based on the belief that the "baseline" would be John 3:16:

> *"Please write as much as you can remember of John 3:16."*

Question 46 and the following three questions were used to see if the respondent could memorize and use Scripture in response to questions:

> *"If someone tells you that Jesus is not God, which Bible verse(s) would you quote as an answer?"*

Question 47:

> *"If someone says that the Bible is not enough, but there must also be other books, how would you answer by quoting the Bible?"*

Question 48:

> *"Which Bible verse(s) would you give to someone who wants to become a Christian?"*

Question 49:

> *"When you are faced with temptation, which Bible verse helps you?"*

Several of the above questions also have reference to other information needs. One answer would often provide insight into several areas of our testing.

Tabulation

All questionnaires were collected for central coding and tabulation. The study was done before computers were readily available, so a hand-tabulation system with codes written on "computer" cards was used. Due to the size of this project, two cards were needed for each respondent.

Tabulations were conducted for each of the eight denominations (districts) in which research was conducted. The total figure is also given, and the totals for churches related to the Church of Christ and to the Evangelical Fellowship are given. This gives eleven sets of data for each question. Each set of data is coded and church groups were only provided with the code for their own group. This safeguarded against undesired comparisons.

Results

The results of the research were far from encouraging concerning the situation of the churches, but on the other hand, the study provided important data for strategy development. In relation to the decision process model presented in chapter 3, most of the churches would be very low on the cognitive dimension, but quite positive on the affective dimension.

It was obvious that the level of Bible knowledge was quite low, and so was the understanding of such key subjects as evangelism and fellowship.

The research also seemed to indicate that the channels of communication used by church leadership were not relevant and effective. The only reading observed by the students involved in the preliminary study of nine churches was Bible reading in church on Sundays. Yet, all the communication from the church headquarters came by letters and printed material, which nobody seemed to read. Radio could be utilized, as the data indicated a fairly high percentage of radio listening by the respondents. But with the relatively low number of Christians, scattered all over the country, radio would be fairly expensive for teaching Christians (but relatively inexpensive for use in evangelism). From other experiments in Thailand we have seen that the audio cassette is an outstanding communications tool for such a purpose.

Based on this study, it was concluded that top priority should be given to the teaching of Christians. That is, use a major part of available resources for an extensive program of Bible teaching. Respondents also indicated this as a main felt need and their willingness and devotion was clear.

This case study has been presented for the primary purpose of illustrating the need for developing good definition of terms and identifying information needs. The definitions were used to identify information needs on which we could base our diagnosis regarding a certain situation. This example also shows a clear line of process from one activity to the next, and how questions on the questionnaire are directly linked to information needs. Such a correspondence between information needs and questions is important for data interpretation and analysis. The presentation here has been very brief to illustrate some selected points, but the study itself was very extensive, with an enormous amount of data collected.

DATA SOURCES

Prior to any survey research, an analysis of secondary data sources will also be conducted. Secondary data is information already gathered for other purposes. It can be data available within the organization or data provided by an external group.

Internal secondary data can be information collected by the organization itself or by a church through a regular monitoring system. It could be data on worship attendance over a period of years, or it could be data available in the church office regarding members and their families. It could also be data collected by an organization through another research project, but data that might now be useful in our present study.

External secondary data can come from a wide variety of sources. Libraries will be primary sources for information as many research reports have been published. Secondary data will also come from syndicated services that deliver research services as a business. For example, media agencies will have data available on readers, listeners, and viewers and a host of other information related to the use of media in a given country. Much secondary data can also be obtained from government departments, including regular census data on the general population.

The primary advantage of secondary data is that it saves cost and time. Many organizations may not be financially capable of conducting extensive research projects on their own.

But there are serious limitations regarding secondary data. Such limitations are usually classified as *data fit problems* and *data accuracy problems*. Secondary data has been collected for other purposes, so categories may not *fit* the need of our present study. If the information needs were very different in the original study and the data categories were different, then the data may range from impossible to use to exact fit. It could be different age groups as well as different periods of time. Our objectives may, for example, call for data from 15–17 years olds, but the data available from a secondary source may cover 13–18 year olds. There could also be a problem regarding time. If the study is three years old, we need to consider if the data is still accurate.

In order to evaluate the accuracy of secondary data, we need first of all to look at the source of the data. It is important to get to the original source rather than just working with a source that has got the data from somewhere else. We also need to look at the purpose of publishing the data. It could have been published as part of a promotional campaign, or it could have been made available by an anonymous source. This does not mean that it is useless, but we need to be careful in using it.

Accuracy can also be established by a careful look at the quality of the research methodology. Such evaluation needs to focus on the sampling plan, how questionnaires were constructed and tested, what were the field collection procedures, and how was the actual data analysis carried out.

Secondary data should be used whenever possible, but we must assure that there is a good fit for the data with our present information needs, and we need to carefully evaluate the accuracy of the data before using it.

6

RESEARCH DESIGN

| Identify Information Needs |
| Determine Sources of Data |
| **Develop Research Design** |
| Design Sampling Plan |

Once we have gone through the initial phases of the research process we can proceed to the actual task of planning the research design. The careful attention given to the development of objectives and information needs will pay off in the design of an appropriate research project. A research design is a plan that will guide the whole research process. It will therefore include instructions on what kind of information that needs to be obtained, from where will you get the data, and what kind of procedures will govern the collection process. In other words it will include the definition of sources for data, sampling plan, and the construction of the data collection form itself.

A first question in the design process relates to the type of research involved. You could call it a classification, and such classification will depend on your objectives and your interest. We can look at it from the perspective of marketing research which relates to the decision making process, or we can look at it from the perspective of communication (media) research.

RESEARCH DESIGN RELATED TO A DECISION-MAKING PROCESS

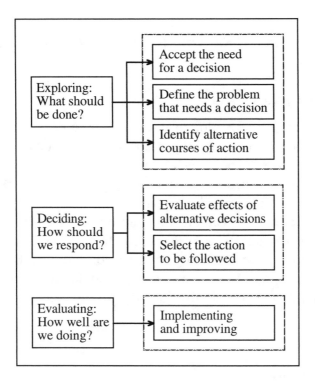

Figure 6. 1
Types of Research and the Decision-Making Process

The classification is here related to the three main areas of a decision-making process: exploring, deciding, and evaluating. The three types can be briefly explained as follows:

1. Exploring: What should be done?
Relate research to the decision problem at hand: defining the situation and identifying options (Exploratory Research).

2. Deciding: How should we respond?

Compare options to decide on the best course of action (Conclusive Research).

3. Evaluating: How well are we doing?

Monitor implementation and provide information for strategy review and possible revision (Performance Monitoring Research).

TYPES OF RESEARCH AS RELATED TO STATED RESEARCH OBJECTIVES

Exploratory Research

The primary interest of exploratory research is to discover opportunities and needs. It may be an analysis of needs in the community surrounding a local church, or it could be a study of an unreached people group. It could also be a study of a certain population as to possible markets for new products. For example, an educational video producer may want to discover the distribution possibilities among home-schoolers in the United States, or it may be a book publisher trying to discover the possibilities of marketing Christian books through secular bookstores in Bangladesh. So the concern is to identify the opportunities and develop an understanding of the possibilities. It would also identify possible alternative courses of action.

Descriptive Research

Descriptive research is in many ways similar to exploratory research, but the primary concern is to get a picture, a snapshot of the situation or context in which we minister. The purpose is to provide an accurate description of the audience to be reached. It can be a study of television viewing patterns of the youth in your community, or it can be a description of actual Bible reading habits among your church members.

Conclusive Research

Managers, pastors and leaders of Christian organizations will often need to select an approach among a number of alternatives. This could be a decision regarding worship songs in the church, which kind and how many times should a song be repeated. A book publisher will want to select a cover design from among a set of alternatives. Conclusive research will, as the name indicates, help to make a final decision before implementation takes place.

Monitoring Research

All leaders need basic ongoing information regarding their ministry. A radio organization will want to know the size and composition of the audience. A pastor will gather regular data on church attendance and church activities to study trends and be aware of approaching problems. A Bible society will keep track of Bible sales to assist them in long-term planning. The secular television industry is dependent on research to know how many people viewed a certain program. The payment for commercials on television is calculated on the basis of the number of viewers.

Causal Research

It is always difficult to be exact regarding cause-and-effect relationships, and consequently we are prone to jump to conclusions. For example, a person may claim that something happened because he or she prayed. The problem is that we do not know if this is true. Others will claim that thousands were converted because of their ministry, yet a closer look may tell us that the real cause of the results was something completely different, maybe the ongoing testimony of a local church, or it could even be caused by political oppression of a minority group. The ministry claiming the results may only have played a very minor role in the total process. Causal research will help us understand which variables actually contributed to the results, and it will help us predict future effects. *Usually multiple causes*

Long-Term Effects

Much research only provides information on short term results, but the real need is to understand the long-term effects and trends. It is more important to see the number of people in church two years after they walked up to the front at an evangelistic crusade than to count the number of those who actually did it. Our research should therefore have a longitudinal perspective where performance is monitored over a long period of time.

Object of Study	Focus of Study
WHO says . . . Source Research	*The Communicator* • interests and opinions • motivations and goals • lifestyle and credibility
. . . WHAT . . . Content Analysis	*The Message Content* • basic content • format of presentation • effects, sounds, visuals
. . . to WHOM . . . Audience Study	*The Audience* • individual characteristics • contextual factors • needs
. . . through WHICH CHANNEL and . . . Media Comparisons	*The Media* • exposure and distribution • comparative analysis • media influence and effects
. . . with WHAT EFFECT Effects Evaluation	*The Results* • cognitive changes • affective changes • behavioral changes

Figure 6. 2
Research Design and Lasswell's Model

RESEARCH DESIGN RELATED TO THE COMMUNICATION MODEL

The communication model can also be a useful context for categorizing research. If we follow the process indicated by the communication model we could identify the following research focus: *the communicator, the audience, the message, the media, the reception situation,* and *the effects.* An appropriate approach would also be to categorize on the basis of the statement by Lasswell in which he suggests that the effects of communication depend on *Who says What to Whom through Which Channel with What Effect.*[1] The approach is illustrated and explained in figure 6.2.

It should be noted that the term media not only refers to the electronic media, or the more popular understanding of the term "The Media." It refers to all channels of communication, including the human body, the pulpit, and various symbols used in a church.

DEFINITION OF IMPORTANT TERMS

There are three terms often used in this material which need definition. Engel describes them as follows:[2]

Error:
— *the extent to which data collected from a subset of a larger population fails to reflect the actual information which would emerge if this larger population were surveyed in entirety. In other words, this is a measure of the inaccuracy which can result from using a sample.*

Bias:
— *inaccuracy in survey data resulting from faulty steps in the research design process itself other than sampling. Examples would be misleading questioning procedures and data interpretation contaminated by a desire to prove a point.*

---

1. Wilbur Schramm and Donald Roberts, *The Process and Effects of Mass Communication.* Revised edition, University of Illinois Press, 1971:84.
2. James F. Engel, *How Can I Get Them to Listen?* Zondervan, 1977:39.

Criteria	Personal Interview	Telephone Interview	Direct Mail
Versatility and Use	• Most versatile • Probes are possible • Can use complex rating scales • Ability to adapt • Can be used in all countries	• Quite flexible • Flow can change • Cannot use complex rating scales • Limited by phone ownership	• Fixed form • Complex scales can be used • Cannot alter • Limited by illiteracy and lack of mail services
Speed of data collection	• Very time-consuming unless many interviewers • Time needed to contact respondent	• Very fast with several calls in an hour • Can be done immediately after an event	• Long time needed to get response • Time interval between design and data return

Response rate	• Response rate influenced by:
	  • not-at-home
	  • refusal to cooperate
	  • personality of interviewer
		• High chance of response where phones available
		• Easy to decline cooperation
		• Voice important to get cooperation
			• Often poor response
			• Depends on perceived benefits
			• Easy to refuse
			• Takes time

Quantity of data collected	• If good rapport established, then extensive data can be obtained • Use of show cards, and material possible	• Limited to a few minutes • Limited use of scales provides less sophisticated data categories	• Good questionnaires can be long, depending on topic • Long questionnaires will reduce response rate
Quality of data obtained	• Enhanced by presence of interviewer • Influenced by interviewer bias and reluctance to respond	• Questionable if sensitive questions are asked • Tend to give more non-committal answers	• Opportunity provided for careful reply • Sensitive data may be inaccurate if not anonymous
Cost of data collection	• Usually most expensive as interviewers need to be paid for time • Very expensive if wide geographic area to be covered	• Cheapest method if phone calls are local • Long-distance calls will be a limitation	• If high response, then relatively inexpensive • Low response expensive • Pay for printing and mailing

Figure 6. 3
Comparing Interview Methods

Research cost:

> — *obviously this refers to the outlays necessitated to collect and analyze data using a particular type of research design.*

Each of these terms will be treated in more detail later. They all influence the accuracy and usefulness of our research.

GETTING THE INFORMATION

Asking Questions of Respondents

expect 50 +9 mne ... real stamp —

The most common type of research is communication with respondents, that is, asking questions. Much of this communication can be informal as used in pretesting and informal information-gathering, but our primary concern here is formalized information-gathering in a survey research project. The interaction with each respondent is a communication event, and it will therefore be subject to all principles of communication if accurate and useful information is to be gathered.

A research design may also call for qualitative data which can be gathered in interviews with a few selected individuals. This can be group interviews where the whole group participate in the response and discussion, or it can be in-depth interviews with an individual where the researcher continues to probe deeper into the responses. *Overlap*

Quantitative research is usually obtained through three different kinds of interviews: personal interview, telephone interview, and mail questionnaires. The chart in figure 6.3 gives a comparison of these three types of interviewing. The approaches can be modified and a certain amount of overlap can occur. For example, the personal interview can be conducted in a group setting where each participant has a self-administered questionnaire which makes it possible to keep anonymity.

	Structured	Unstructured
Undisguised	1	3
Disguised	2	4

Figure 1. 1.
Variations of Question Design and Structures

Structured vs. Unstructured Approaches

We shall in a following chapter look at the actual design of questionnaires and the formulation of questions, but let us here briefly look at different approaches we can take to the planning of questions. Figure 6.4 provides a diagram of four basic categories of questions.[3]

Structured questions refer to questions where the respondent will either not have any alternatives, or will have to choose between certain alternatives provided on the questionnaire. A disguised question is a question where the purpose of the question is not directly obvious to the respondent.

Example of Structured, Undisguised Question (1):

Do you feel that your church needs more or less congregational singing during the Sunday morning worship service? (check one)
__ *Needs more*
__ *Needs less*
__ *Neither more nor less*
__ *No opinion*

This type of question is easy to administer in the field, and it is easy to enter into a computer program for tabulation. A possible negative would be lack of definition or not enough alternatives.

Example of Structured, Disguised Question (2):

Would you say that most of the people in your church would prefer more or less congregational singing during the Sunday morning worship service? (check one)
__ *Prefer more*
__ *Prefer less*
__ *Neither more nor less*
__ *No opinion*

Such an approach will avoid creating embarrassment on behalf of the respondent if he or she is not prepared to give their own opinion. By for-

---

3. Ibid., p. 72ff.

mulating it in a third-person format, the respondent will be more free to answer. The assumption is that the respondents will actually give their own answers.

Example of the Unstructured, Undisguised Question (3)

What are your feelings about congregational singing during the Sunday morning service? Would you like more singing, less singing, or what? _____

This kind of question gives the respondent an opportunity to give a response in his or her own words. After the answer is given, the interviewer can then probe deeper to get a more complete answer. The approach has a number of advantages, which we shall look at later, but it also makes it extremely difficult to tabulate results and develop tendencies.

Example of Unstructured, Disguised Question (4)

This type of question requires significant creativity. A whole range of projective techniques can be used. The idea is to have the respondent see himself or herself in a situation and then respond. It could be through the use of pictures, or it could be a sentence completion technique where the person is asked to complete a sentence such as,

"As far as the singing in church Sunday morning is concerned, my feeling is that _____.

Anthropologists have in a number of situations found such sentence completion techniques very helpful when they try to understand the underlying feelings for certain types of behavior.

ALTERNATIVE TYPES OF RESEARCH DESIGN

Before we proceed with our development of survey research methods, let us briefly look at some alternative approaches to information gathering.

Some of these may be used in conjunction with a survey research project to add other dimensions. Some of the types mentioned here may also use questionnaires for data collection.

Observing Behavior

In our daily lives we constantly observe reality to gather information. From what we see, we make our diagnosis and interpret events. Similarly, we learn much about God by observing his acts of creation and continuous sustaining power of the universe. People look at people and develop opinions about them. In research we can learn much from the observation of behavior or the results of such behavior. If accurate information can be obtained by observation, it will not be necessary to conduct survey interviews.

If I am to find out what is the most popular painting in an exhibition, all I need to do is to observe people's behavior, that is, how many and how long do they stand in front of a particular painting. Or, I could come after closing time and see where the floor is most dirty. I can also observe the popularity of traditional drama by observing the response of people in the audience. On the other hand, we cannot through observation determine the motivations and attitudes behind certain behavior, and it would be next to impossible to gather knowledge about people's awareness level through observation.

Certain types of information will have to be gathered through observation, and a trained observer can gather important data. Sometimes it is done unobtrusively, that is, the objects of the study are not aware of research being conducted.

In any case, it is important to have a structure for the gathering of data so that the data can be tabulated and categorized. Often data from observation will provide a qualitative dimension to data gathered through other means. A researcher conducting personal interviews in a village or in a home will also be able to observe certain items that can be part of the research study.

Focus Groups

Communication and marketing research agencies often use focus groups to test products and commercials. A focus group is a group depth interview with a small group of people. It is conducted by a trained moderator, and the interview is loosely structured. There will be a careful organization of topics to be discussed, but the interview setting itself provides flexibility for exploring a topic in depth.

The best size for a focus group is ten to twelve participants. Smaller groups tend to be dominated by a few of the respondents, while larger groups give less opportunity for all to participate. All participants will be carefully screened ahead of time, and there will usually be exact specifications regarding the selection of participants.

The skills of the moderator is of prime importance. He or she needs to maintain a high degree of interaction among group members, so a primary role is to stimulate interaction within the group rather than conducting individual interviews in the group.

Focus groups can be used for numerous purposes in Christian communication. It can, for example, be exploratory research to discover needs of a specific audience, or it can be conclusive research to select a book cover from among several alternatives. A focus group interview can therefore add significant qualitative information to our overall knowledge of a topic or of an audience.

Test Groups and Experiments

Experimental designs aimed at studying the responses of a group of people to a certain approach or product is an approach used widely in marketing research. In a test group we control other inputs, and then measure the responses to the object under study. A test group can consist of just a few people, or it can be a whole city. It can be one local church or it can be a whole denomination. The main issue is that we are testing products or approaches on a smaller group before making the services available to all.

If a new program is to be designed, it would be advisable to carry out a controlled experiment. Various types of products can be tested in both controlled group settings and in real market situations. The process is similar and will usually consist of the following few steps:

Step 1: Test the group to obtain baseline information
Step 2: Expose the group to the new product or approach
Step 3: Test the group to obtain information on new position
Step 4: Compare pre-test and post-test results.

Experiments tend to suffer from a number of measurement biases, and they can be quite costly. On the other hand, it may be far more costly to start a new program that has not been tested well through experiments.

New programs can be significantly improved if one or more pilot programs are carried out. Pilot programs are experiments in which we carefully evaluate the results. Another benefit of a pilot program is that we are free to fail.

Case Studies

Case studies are well-known from church growth research in which successful churches have been analyzed. Similarly, significant work has been done on analyzing testimonies from people who have left one religion and joined another. Much information regarding communication and development has been learned through case studies related to new innovations. In anthropological studies, societies are analyzed and studied.

Case studies will often provide qualitative data for a study and provide many of the underlying motives and dynamics of a movement. It is therefore recommended that survey research will be enhanced by a few selected case studies that provide a more qualitative picture and a more comprehensive description of the situation.

Simulation

In a simulation we try to create an environment that would be like a real-world situation. A good illustration is the use of a flight simulator in training airplane pilots. They are "flying" the simulator where all possible situations can occur and they are gaining experience in how to respond in emergency situations.

For the marketing manager, computer programs are available for working through different alternative solutions to a certain market phenomena.

A simple simulation would be using a spreadsheet to study possible effects on the financial viability of an organization if there is a long-term change in the dollar exchange rate.

Another approach would be the use of role play in which expected behavior can be observed if certain circumstances arise. This could be part of a training program in evangelism. At a recent course of the Asian Institute of Christian Communication, we simulated situations where the participants would meet their colleagues after a long absence.

Simulation can then be a good approach to testing alternative solutions to a situation or a problem.

Selecting an Approach

The question is, Which type of research design would be most appropriate to your need? Often we find that a combination of approaches is necessary to provide a design that would meet the requirements of our particular need.

7

Survey Sampling

Develop Research Design
Design Sampling Plan
Construct Data Collection Form

Why sampling? We use sampling because it is not normally possible to take a census where information is collected from everybody in a population. In a sample, we choose a subset from a larger group to represent the whole group. Sampling has been developed as a very refined science in which error can be measured and we can make quite accurate predictions on the basis of a sample selected according to the rules of sampling.

Without sampling we would not be able to conduct survey research as we know it today. Sampling is used extensively in research, and we all know it from news broadcasts, where opinion polls on political convictions and intentions are reported. Usually, the reporter will conclude the report by saying, *This was based on 1843 interviews* or something like that. The question is then, how can so few people out of a population of millions be accurate within a few plus/minus percentage points? This chapter will give an introduction to sampling and seek to provide the information the reader will need to conduct some basic sampling activities. For more sophisticated samples, the reader is advised to study some of the books referred to in the bibliography or consult an experienced researcher or statistician.

The basic concept of sampling is not too difficult to understand. It is a matter of selecting a smaller group from a larger group to represent all. It could, for example, be the selection of a group of churches to study a whole denomination. If the group is chosen according to the rules of sampling, we will be able to state how accurate the estimates can be said to be.

The ability to generalize from the subset is based on mathematical formulas. We can say that a sample, properly chosen, will be able to provide an accurate picture of the larger group within measurable error. Sampling error is a measure of how much results obtained from a sample will deviate from the whole group.

WHY SAMPLING

Sampling has several major benefits as over against taking a census, in which everybody is chosen.

1. *Sampling saves money*. This is probably the most obvious reason. The cost of one single interview is quite high if interviewers are to be paid by the hour. Imagine what it would cost to interview a million people. A sample might only require a few hundred. There will also be savings in printing of questionnaires and in the tabulation of results.

2. *Sampling saves time*. The interviewing process itself takes time, and the difference between four hundred interviews and four hundred thousand, for example, is enormous. Beyond the actual interviewing time, we will also save time for tabulation and data analysis.

3. *Sampling is more accurate*. The primary reason that a sample can provide more accurate findings is that a census will have more nonsampling errors. Nonsampling errors are errors related to the research process but not part of the sampling process. For example, a census will require more interviewers, and for each person added, we run the risk of adding bias to the interviewing process. It is

much more difficult to train and give quality control to a large group than to a small group of interviewers. Another potential area of nonsampling error for a census is that it takes much longer time, so the phenomenon we are studying may actually change due to some contextual factors during the interview process.

4. *Sampling avoids contamination of the study population.* This is important when we want to take pre- and post-tests. If the whole group has already been exposed to the topic in a pretest, their attitudes and behavior may have changed due to the test. This is called *contamination* of the sample. We cannot expect a post-test to be accurate in the same way as it would be if taken from a *non-contaminated* sample. Sampling methods make it possible to have different, but matched samples for pre- and post-tests.

SOME SAMPLING CONCEPTS

Concept of Representativeness

The basic requirement of all samples is that they are representative. That is, the sample must be representative of the total group (universe/population) which we are surveying. In order to achieve representativeness, we need to both select the appropriate sampling method and engage in creative sampling design.

Concept of Randomness

In a random sample, every person in the total population must have a known chance of being selected for the sample. It is not a haphazard or convenient way of selecting the respondents, but a carefully designed plan that will give each person a known chance of being selected. It is only when a sample is chosen by random that we can apply the findings to the total population, and we can do that within measurable error limits. It will never be possible to have a sample that precisely mirrors the total population, but we will always strive for that.

There are two basic questions that need to be asked before selecting respondents for a random sample. The first question deals with accuracy, or stated in research terms, how much *statistical error* is allowed. This is a question for management to decide. How much error will be tolerated in the estimates that will be derived from the study? Often we are satisfied with a +/- 5% error which means that obtained results may differ within these limits from results that might have been obtained from the total population. If such a sample would show 60% for a certain position, then we can statistically say that the true results will be between 57% and 63%. The larger the sample, the less statistical error will be the result.

The other question relates to *confidence level.* That is how confident we are that the actual results fall within the error limits. If we want to be 95% confident, then we need to establish a 95% confidence level for the sample. In other words, we will be 95% sure that the accurate results will fall within the error limits. Again, the larger the sample, the more confident we can be. Statistical charts have been developed for selecting sample size based on statistical error and confidence levels.

Definition of Sampling Terms

The language of sampling has, as already seen, a number of technical terms. The key terms used in defining a research sample are *element, population, sampling unit, sampling frame*, and *study population.*

An *Element* is a unit we are seeking information about. It is therefore the basis of analysis. The most common elements in sampling are individuals, but it could also be products, churches, or families.

The research *Population* is the aggregate of all the elements defined prior to selection of the sample. It is also called the *universe*. A population is defined in terms of four criteria: *elements, sampling units, extent,* and *time*. Let us look at a couple of examples.

If we were to make a survey to discover study problems encountered by female students at Fuller Seminary School of World Mission, we could define the research population (universe) as follows:

1. Element   Fuller Seminary Student
2. Sampling units   School of World Mission, then Female
3. Extent   Pasadena Campus
4. Time   January 22–31, 1996

The research population (universe) for a survey designed to measure retail sales of Bibles could be defined as follows:

1. Element   Bibles
2. Sampling units   Christian Bookstore, Secular Bookstores
3. Extent   Pasadena
4. Time   January 22–31, 1996

A *Sampling Unit* is the element or elements available for selection during the sampling process. In simple, single-stage sampling the sampling units and the elements are the same, but when more complex sampling procedures are utilized, then sampling units and elements are different for the purposes of selection. In both cases above, we reach the elements indirectly through the sampling units. In practice we often go through several stages in the selection of the sample, as we shall see in the cases provided later.

The *Sampling Frame* is some kind of list of all the sampling units available for selection in the sampling process. It is from this list the actual sample is drawn. We often need considerable creativity to arrive at an appropriate sampling frame. A frame can be a class list, or a list of all students in a seminary. It could be a local church membership roster or a telephone book. In some cases it can be a map where we select on the basis on some geographical criteria. In many countries we do not have accurate lists that can be used as sampling frames, so other methods are needed. For all research projects, we need as close a fit as possible between the actual population and the sampling frame.

The *Study Population* is the aggregate of elements from which the sample is actually drawn. For several reasons, the total population will not be available for selection at the time of drawing the sample. If we will be interviewing all members of a household, then we will always miss some. There will be those who are temporarily in hospital, traveling, or away at college. Or, if we are using a phone book for selection of the sample, then those without a phone will be excluded. The study population will therefore be smaller than the actual population.

SAMPLING PROCEDURES

[handwritten: cannot be applied to total]

There are two basic categories of sampling procedures, *probability sampling* and *nonprobability sampling*. We have already discussed the term *random sample*. Randomness is needed for a probability sample. In a probability sample, all elements have a known chance of being selected. In a *nonprobability sampling* process, the selection of the sample elements is based in part on the judgment of the researcher. Not everybody in the population will have a chance of being selected, and we are therefore unable to calculate statistical sampling error in a nonprobability sample. There are several different sampling types for each category as indicated on figure 7.1.

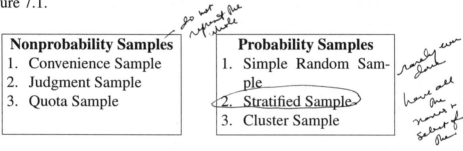

Nonprobability Samples	**Probability Samples**
1. Convenience Sample	1. Simple Random Sample
2. Judgment Sample	2. Stratified Sample
3. Quota Sample	3. Cluster Sample

[handwritten notes around figure: do not repeat while; rarely done; have all one names of select one]

Figure 7. 1
Sampling Procedures

Convenience Sample

A convenience sample is a nonprobability sample where the researcher simply selects those that are conveniently available and willing to participate. It can be walking down the street and asking whoever comes by, or it could be selecting Indian church leaders who are presently studying on a seminary campus in the United States to represent all Indian church leaders. Obviously, they will not be representative of the total population unless they have been defined as such. A seminary professor may also be tempted to use students as a convenient way of selecting a sample.

Convenience samples can be most useful in the exploratory phase of a study, and we can use it extensively for pretesting needs, but we cannot use it for the purpose of arriving at estimates concerning the whole population.

Judgment Sample

Judgment samples, also called purposive samples, are selected on the basis of what a certain expert thinks is appropriate for the study. The judgment will be based on experience and knowledge about the population. Often extensive preliminary study is conducted before judgment is applied to sample selection. The selection of an individual for the study must be based on a knowledge of that particular person's representativeness of the total group.

We can never be sure if a judgment sample is truly representative and no statistical measure of error can be applied. On the other hand, a judgment sample will be more accurate than a convenience sample, and in some cases more useful that a random sample.

Quota Sample

In a quota sample, steps are taken to select the sample in such a way that it represents specific subgroups. The example could be a church denomination. Let us say the denomination has 300 small rural churches with a total membership of 4500. There are also 10 medium size churches in towns with a total of 3000 members, and, finally, there are two large churches with a combined membership of 4000 members. If we were to choose the sample by selecting churches through a simple random approach we may miss the two large churches altogether. A quota sample will require selection of members from each of the three categories of churches, possibly an equal number from each category. Results can then be compared between these churches as well as giving a comprehensive picture of the whole denomination.

In other types of quota samples, the field interviewers may be asked to fill quotas so an equal number of male and female respondents are chosen, or they could be required to fulfill specific age-level quotas. It will be important in such situations to have carefully prepared interviewer guides so that the selection can be controlled according the research objectives.

Simple Random Sample

In a simple random sample all members of a population should have an equal chance of being selected. An example of this would be to write names of all members of a church on small pieces of paper, put them in a bag, and then draw the necessary numbers out of the bag. This will be a simple random sample. In practice this is often not possible, and, as mentioned above, there will be differences between the total population and the study population.

The selection of numbers in a random sample will depend on how accurate the estimates will need to be. Based on accepted statistical error and level of confidence the actual number can be decided. The following chart gives an illustration of the numbers needed for samples with tolerated error between 1% and 7% and with either 95% or 99% confidence levels.

Those returned

Error Which Can Be Tolerated	Sample Size and Desired Confidence	
	95%	99%
1%	9,604	16,587
2%	2,401	4,147
3%	1,067	1,843
4%	600	1,037
5%	384	663
6%	267	461
7%	196	339

Figure 7. 2
Illustration of Sample Size[1]

only significant

Market Research

out of any number 171,00 or 2 million whether

As can be seen from the illustration in figure 7.2, a certain knowledge of statistics is very helpful. This book is being written, though, in such a way that only minimal statistical knowledge is required. The suggestion is therefore that you use the formulas worked out by the experts and use the tables that have been made available in various books on statistics.

---

1. James F. Engel, *How Can I Get Them to Listen?* Zondervan, 1977:55.

Stratified Sample

A stratified sample is a random sample in which selection is based on an approach different from a simple random sample. The total population is divided into stratas before actual selection of elements take place. A stratified sample is then similar to a quota sample in the sense that the elements are defined within specific groups, but the selection of actual respondents is by random selection.

One approach is to take a map of a city, divide it into a number of squares. Each square is given a number, and a number of squares will then be randomly selected, then houses can be selected, and finally the individual within the house. This is a multi-stage selection process which is often used as a practical way of obtaining a random sample that is both representative and practically within reach of the interviewers. If the stratas have been defined by any measure of expert judgment and not by randomness, then we can, of course, only make our estimates for that particular strata. On the other hand, this will in many cases be an appropriate approach to arrive at useful data.

Cluster Sample

A cluster sample is similar to a stratified sample. In cluster sampling the elements are divided into mutually exclusive and collectively exhaustive groups. We then select a random sample of these groups.

STEPS IN SAMPLING PROCESS

We now come to the actual process of selecting the sample. There are several steps to go through.

1. *Define Group to be Studied: Population*. The population itself will be defined in terms of elements, sampling units, extent, and time as described earlier in this chapter.
2. *Identify Source of Names: Sampling Frame*. Identification of a sampling frame is the selection of a list of names or the preparation of some other kind of selection basis such as a city map.
3. *Determine Sample Size*. Sample size will be determined on the basis of the required accuracy of estimates, and the cost involved in

obtaining the data. The bigger the sample, the higher the cost will
be.

4. *Decide on Sampling Procedure*. The research objectives will to a
   large extent determine which sampling procedure should be chosen. Should it be a probability sampling method or a nonprobability
   sampling method?   *Creative*

5. *Select Actual Respondents: The Sample*. Finally, the sample will be
   physically selected. This will be done from the sample frame, and
   various approaches can be used. For example, a table of random
   numbers can be utilized, or we can simply draw lots.

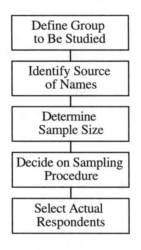

Figure 7. 3
Steps in Sampling Process

*How select
One Sample ?*

CASE STUDY: SELECTING A SAMPLE FOR RADIO RESEARCH
PROJECT IN THAILAND

The purpose and objectives of the following research project has been
referred to earlier in this book.[2] The purpose was stated as follows:

2. Viggo B. Søgaard, "Product Testing of Living Gospel of Mark in Thai." Unpublished
   research report, 1976.

The purpose of the research project is to have a close look at the present as well as potential audience of VOP in order to be as effective as possible in programming, and be able to integrate the ministry in a meaningful and comprehensive strategy together with churches and other media ministries.

Specific objectives were listed as follows:

1. *To study radio listening habits, station and program preference by the audience.*
2. *To determine the size of present listenership to VOP programs.*
3. *To determine effectiveness of individual radio program series.*
4. *To gather demographic data on present audience.*
5. *To uncover felt needs by target audience.*
6. *To obtain value ratings by the target audience.*
7. *To do a spiritual segmentation and understanding study of the target audience by comparing listeners to non-listeners.*

Research Design

In order to project reliable findings to the total audience, it was decided to gather probability data, which again demands random sampling. In a probability sample, all members of the research universe should have a known chance of being selected as respondents. This, in turn, demands the existence of some kind of listing of all members of the universe. Such lists did not exist in Thailand. There was no accurate information, no phone books, no directories, and no census information available for our use. Furthermore, this was the first study of its kind directed by this author.

The process of gathering probability data would, as is usually the case in developing countries, involve considerable creative thinking and planning. The method chosen was a stratified random sample. In a stratified sample we could use other criteria for respondent selection than a list of names.

Furthermore, it was decided that information-gathering was to be conducted through personal interviews. There were no telephones that could be used, and mail surveys required a reasonable and well-functioning postal system. This did not really exist in villages. A major part of the research universe were illiterates, and this would further complicate the survey. Personal interviewing was therefore seen as the only alternative.

Radio listening in Thailand was at that time usually a "family affair." The houses are open with thin bamboo or wooden walls and no windows. When the radio is on, everybody in the house will listen. The same is true for neighboring houses. For our research, we would therefore choose households rather than individuals. The heads of households or the most senior person present would be interviewed.

Sampling

As indicated above, sampling usually involves a number of complications in a developing country. For practical reasons two areas were chosen for the study: the Chiangmai area in the North and the Narkhonsawan area in the central part of the country. These two areas were believed to be representative of the audience of VOP. Earlier studies and letter response seemed to confirm this decision. By choosing these two areas on the basis of expert judgment, it was realized that resulting statistics could only be used for these two areas. On the other hand, we were satisfied that the representativeness of the areas were such that we could apply the basic findings to other areas as well.

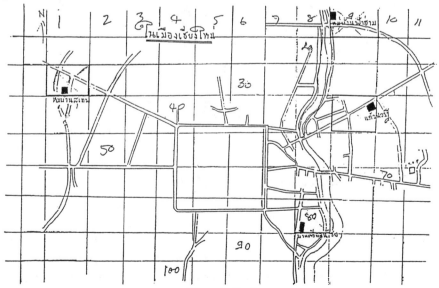

Figure 7. 4
Grid Indicating Selection of Strata in Towns

It was decided to use a sample size of 400. This should give enough accuracy for our purpose. A computerized size for a 5% statistical error and a confidence level of 95% would be 384 respondents. As both rural areas and towns were to be included, the sample of 400 was divided into sixteen stratas of twenty-five respondents. Four strata were to be chosen from each of the two towns and four strata from the rural areas surrounding the two towns. Maps were then used to select the individual strata:

The map in figure 7.4 is from Chiangmai, but the same method was used for Narkhonsawan. Grids were drawn on the maps and the four strata were chosen randomly. In a particular area chosen, the main road from the city center would be located and every second house in the stratum would be chosen as sites of interview until the quota of twenty-five interviews were obtained.

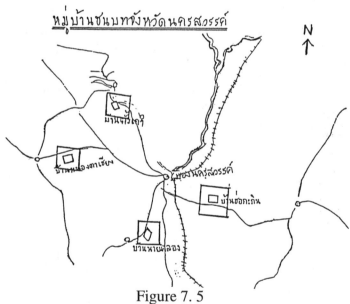

Figure 7. 5
Map Indicating Selection of Strata in Rural Area

A similar system was used for the rural areas as illustrated on figure 7.5. On this map, all roads leading out of the city were numbered. Among these numbers, four would be selected by random (drawing lots). For each road a number between one and ten was then randomly selected. If, for example, number seven was selected on road number four, then the seventh village on that road would be selected, counting from the edge of town. In each village every second house would be selected until the quota of twenty-five had been obtained.

CASE STUDY: SELECTING A SAMPLE FOR STUDENT RESEARCH PROJECT, RELATED TO PRODUCT TESTING AND THE DEVELOPMENT OF A MARKETING STRATEGY

This present study deals with the topic of testing media products, as well as a study of student needs, interests, and Bible awareness. The general purpose was to conduct a product test on the Living Gospel of Mark in the Thai language, in order to determine its potential market in terms of responsive audience segments, and to gather data for a meaningful marketing strategy. The Gospel of Mark was the first book translated by Living Bibles International into Thai, so the project had a certain pretesting value.[3]

Research Objectives
The following specific objectives were given:

1. *To have a pretested model for testing similar selections.*
2. *To obtain demographic data on the potential market in terms of geographic location, social level, age, and religion.*
3. *To test the attitude of the audience to the present product in terms of price range, cover design, title, printing, pictures, and general acceptability.*
4. *To determine problems and felt needs of the audience and to test how far the Living Mark is conceived to be able to meet these needs.*
5. *To gather certain data on perceived comprehension and the emotive value of the text.*
6. *To obtain specific data on previous Bible knowledge and understanding by the target audience.*
7. *To test the attitude to Christians by the target audience.*

---

3. Viggo Søgaard, "Product Testing of Living Gospel of Mark in Thai." Unpublished research report, 1976.

Preliminary Information
At the start of the research project the organization supplied certain information that should help in research design and areas of testing. Among these were the so-called distinguishing features of a Living Bible.

Furthermore, the aim of the translation had been to reach non-Christian youth, and they should not look at it as a Bible, but as a book that answers life-problems. The language aimed at was a style like that of a personal letter.

Marketing was expected to be through both Christian and secular bookstores, evangelistic agencies, and by mobilizing churches and Christians in evangelistic outreach.

Parameters for Research Design
In order to set the parameters for the research project, a number of interviews and conferences were conducted. The observations listed below were made during this initial stage of research design. It should be noted that several of these points may have changed so that the situation today may vary from these observations.

1. *The translators of the Living Gospel of Mark in Thai have set their aim at people who have received seventh grade of education.*
2. *Apart from the present student body, the majority of the people in Thailand have not studied beyond fourth grade.*
3. *According to general observation, people whose formal education is not beyond fourth grade do not regularly read books or magazines.*
4. *Advertising in newspapers and magazines by the OMF Publishers are being responded to by young people between twelve and twenty-two years of age with and average of 17 years old.*
5. *The C&MA correspondence course students have an average age of 14. The vast majority of students are between ten and twenty years of age.*
6. *Every Home Crusade (also a literature program) has found that the average age of those returning the decision cards is twelve years.*
7. *Among those enrolled in another correspondence school, operated by Presbyterians, over 68% are students.*

8. *According to information obtained from the Bible society, colporteurs can only sell Bible portions to the "general public" because they are in sets together with other books, and they are sold at an extremely cheap price. Three books for one Baht. They are not necessarily read.*

9. *At present colporteurs are finding that Christian literature is selling much better when sold to students in schools.*

10. *The annual OMF competition books, which are sold in schools, have much higher sales than other Christian books.*

11. *The Thai Bible Society is receiving constant requests from schools to put Bibles in their libraries.*

12. *The price of the Living Gospel of Mark in Thai is 3 Baht, which is about three times the equivalent of a Bible selection from the Bible society.*

13. *Students seem to be willing to and able to pay more for books – that is, if they feel the value of it justifies the price.*

14. *The selling of books in schools has been most successful when done through a teacher.*

15. *A special "Student Bible" has been requested by many Christian workers.*

16. *The official student addresses are erratic, and most do not change their addresses when they move off to school somewhere else.*

These general observations clearly pointed to the youth of Thailand as the major market for The Living Bible, and in particular the student population. This also coincided with the general objectives of the sponsoring organization.

Research Design

In order to avoid biased answers and complications in interpretation, it was decided to use two matched samples. Information needed for objectives 1–5 would be collected from sample one, and information needed for objectives 6–7 would be collected from sample two.

Based on the preliminary study, it was decided to limit the research to students, and to conduct the actual research in schools. Furthermore, it was decided to start with fifth grade and test up through college level.

The interviews would be in groups of ten, but they would use individual, self-administered questionnaires. The individual student would be anonymous, yet we would know school and class.

The Living Gospel of Mark would be tested on sample one. There would be four stages to the test, resembling the stages of the process involved in buying the book in a book shop: (a) catching the attention, (b) the immediate communication of the cover, (c) perception after quickly skipping through it, and then, (d) attitude after having read it, or part of it. The four sections or stages would then be as follows,

Section 1: Rating the Living Mark – by sight only – among eleven alternatives, including Christian books, politics, love stories, and others.

Section 2: An evaluation of the Living Mark based on its front cover only.

Section 3: Evaluation of the Living Mark after one minute of skipping through it.

Section 4: Evaluation of the Living Mark after having had it for a few days.

Sections 1–3 would be conducted in the same session, and section 4 would be conducted a few days later.

Sample two, which was tested on general attitudes and felt needs, as well as biblical understanding and attitudes to Christians was completed in one session.

Research Sample
Due to the fact that no listing of names and addresses were available for the selection of our research sample, it was decided to base sampling on schools.

1. *Accurate listing of schools with size and number of classes were obtained from various educational departments.*
2. *Schools were then randomly selected.*
3. *Two classes were randomly selected from each school. If, for example, grade 8 was chosen in a particular school, then class 8A would*

*be chosen for sample one and 8B for sample two. This should pro-
vide good matched samples.*

4. *From each class ten students were randomly selected for inclusion
in the sample.*

These two case studies have been presented as illustrations of sample
design in countries where special conditions require a creative approach
to sampling. In both cases, proper sampling procedures have been followed.

8

CONSTRUCTION OF QUESTIONNAIRES

Design Sampling Plan
Construct Data Collection Form
Data Collection in the Field

After all the preliminary work is over, we can finally begin to construct the questionnaire. Careful work on the objectives and information needs will pay off well at this stage.

FUNCTION OF THE QUESTIONNAIRE

A questionnaire functions as the link between the information needs and the respondents. It is a formalized way of collecting data from respondents, but, due to possible measurement errors, the help of an experienced researcher is needed to design the questionnaire. There are no series of steps, principles, or guidelines which guarantee an effective and efficient questionnaire. It is both an art and a scientific undertaking.

Questionnaires are used widely and the reader will have come across both good and poor questionnaires. This may have been in a hotel room or in a restaurant, in a shopping mall or on the street. If a questionnaire is poorly made and it has a measurement error, the collected data will be useless, or even lead to wrong decisions. The researcher will therefore continue to ask himself or herself the questions: *Am I getting accurate information? Am I getting valuable information?* And, *Is the question measuring what it is supposed to measure?*

Figure 8. 1
Function of Data Collection Form

An illustration of how different wordings of a question gave different results is provided by the Survey Research Center at the University of Michigan.[1] A consumer survey was conducted to measure attitudes toward a gasoline price increase. Half of the sample was asked, "Are you in favor of the proposed standby gasoline tax, starting with 5 cents and rising to 50 cents, which will be imposed if we do not meet conservation goals?" Twenty-seven percent of the respondents favored the tax, while

---

1. F. Thomas Juster, "A Note on Energy Policy and Automobile Demand," in *Economic Outlook USA.* Summer vol. 4, number 3.

65% were against. The other half of the sample were asked, "If the United States had to choose between becoming dependent on uncertain foreign oil supplies or curbing gasoline use with rising taxes, which would you favor?" The result was that 71% was in favor of higher taxes and only 13% opposed the proposal. We see that the first question does not give an explicit alternative, so the implicit alternative is higher or lower taxes. The question to the second group offered an explicit choice, higher taxes versus dependence on foreign oil supplies. So the results can be rather meaningless if a preference question is asked without realistic alternatives.

Similarly, we might ask a person, "Would you like to learn to read, if this was possible?" The answer would probably be affirmative. On the other hand, if we asked "Would you be interested in attending evening literacy classes, or would you prefer to be home with the family in the evenings?" the results would probably be very different, as many people would like to be able to read, but they do not want to pay the price.

In a tribal village in Pakistan I asked the leaders, "How many in this village can read?" The answer was, "Most of the children." This answer was a puzzle, as only one of the children went to school. After further questioning it became clear that the real meaning of their answer was, "If they had the opportunity, they could learn to read."

STEPS IN QUESTIONNAIRE DESIGN

On the following pages a number of steps are suggested for the construction of a questionnaire. We need to consider (1) the main components of a questionnaire, (2) the questions themselves, (3) the format for response, (4) how to phrase and sequence questions, and finally (5) work on the physical layout of the form itself.

QUESTIONNAIRE COMPONENTS

A questionnaire will have the following components:

1. Identification data   — numbers etc.
2. Instructions
3. Introduction   — reason for doing this — value

4. Questions to be asked ⌐ *informatic needs*
5. Demographic data - *Cross tabulate*
   — *by groups or range*

Identification Data

Each questionnaire will have a number which will be needed for control at
the time of tabulation. On anonymous questionnaires, the number will
probably be added after the questionnaire has been returned. For personal
interviews, the form will also have space for writing date and time of
interview, interviewer name, and possibly also the location of the interview. In some instances, there will also be a need for name and address of
respondent.

Instructions

On questionnaires to be used in personal interviews, instructions are provided for the interviewer to follow so that all interviews can be conducted
in exactly the same way. For a telephone interview, for example, the same
introduction will need to be given, and the interviewer will be instructed
to start the conversation in the same way each time. If it is a self-administered questionnaire, the instructions will seek to help the respondent on
how to complete the questionnaire so that it will result in accurate data.
On such a self-administered questionnaire, the instructions will probably
come after the introduction itself, and there may be a need to give instructions at several places on the questionnaire if special rating scales are
being introduced. A few words of encouragement will also be helpful on
long questionnaires to inspire the respondent to complete the process.

Introduction

In all interviewing, we are asking the respondent to give us some of his or
her valuable time and to provide us with important information. The questionnaire will therefore seek to gain the cooperation of the respondent.
This is a communication situation, and the respondent must see the time
given to answering questions as being important to him or her. Sometimes
a sentence or two is enough, but at other times a whole covering letter or

page will be needed. Such an introduction may be written by a bishop or a church leader. The respondent must see a reason or purpose for the interview to be willing to cooperate. Careful preparation of the introduction is therefore very important to achieve a high response rate.

Questions to be Asked

This will form the main body of the questionnaire and most of this chapter is devoted to the design of good questions. The questions will need to be prepared in such a way that the necessary data will be obtained and the need for information met.

Demographic Data

A questionnaire will usually have a number of demographic questions. These are for classification purposes, and usually such questions are put at the end of the form. If they are put at the beginning, the form can easily be seen as a kind of interrogation and the respondent will be much more guarded in providing accurate responses. Typical classification data are sex, age, education, and income.

At the time of designing questions, we need to consider entry of data into the computer and subsequent tabulation, and how we can reduce extra work with editing. It is therefore best to provide choices that have already been established for categories of demographic data. Instead of asking, "What is your age?" and then leave a blank, it is much more helpful to give choices such as:

(1) __ below 20 years
(2) __ 21–35 years
(3) __ 36–50 years
(4) __ 51–65 years
(5) __ more than 65 years

The response format to the question is pre-coded so that at the time of data entry, only one figure needs to be entered into the computer, and the data can be divided into five different groups. Choices as suggested above are also less intimidating than if you ask for specific personal details.

DESIGNING A QUESTIONNAIRE

The preparation of a questionnaire may seem like a scientific or technical process, but it is also an art where the communication skills of the researcher will be tested. If we approach the work from a receptor-oriented communication perspective, we will constantly have the respondent in mind and seek to communicate with that person in a nice and polite manner. There is no need to let the questions sound like an interrogation. The questions need to be presented in a conversational manner which provides a pleasing atmosphere for the interview or the filling out of a form.

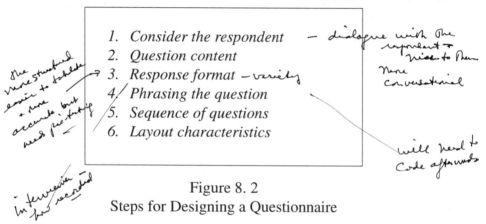

1. Consider the respondent
2. Question content
3. Response format
4. Phrasing the question
5. Sequence of questions
6. Layout characteristics

Figure 8. 2
Steps for Designing a Questionnaire

There is no clear cut process or steps that must be followed. Pretesting will constantly improve the questions and the approach. The above questions are interrelated and will not necessarily be followed in the order given here, and during the design process the researcher will constantly refer back to the information needs to which the questions must relate.

Consider the Respondent

The interview is like any other communication situation where we will meet a wide variety of people. The respondents will all be different and we need to develop approaches applicable to the different situations. A clear description of the respondents from demographic as well as social and cultural perspectives will help, and an understanding of the educational level should influence the language used as well as the level of sophistication used in rating scales and response systems. All of this is aimed at establishing rapport with the respondents in order to gain their cooperation.

We need to consider the respondent's *ability* to answer. Will the respondent be able to provide the information we are seeking? Maybe the topic is one on which *they have no information* or no experience. Researchers have found that people tend to try to answer questions regarding topics on which they do not have information if they think that they ought to have the information. This could be a question in which we ask somebody about his or her religion, or to compare religions. They may feel embarrassed if they cannot answer. Correct phrasing of a question will help solve such a problem.

The respondent may also be *forgetful*. Questionnaires frequently ask questions about things we have forgotten. The further we are from an event, the more we tend to forget the details and the sequence of events. Many research studies have sought to investigate an event after it has taken place and this gives complications. For example, several studies have tried to identify influences that have helped people become Christians. Unless the research is very carefully handled people tend to remember only the last or most prominent event and therefore may give an incomplete picture of the process. People may remember the first car they purchased, but not the second. So when asking questions that demand recall of events, special skills are needed in questionnaire design. There may be a need for certain aids or stimulation to assist in the recollection or ordering of events.

The respondent may also be *unwilling* to respond. There are a number of possible reasons for such unwillingness. First of all, the person may feel that it is not the business of others to ask such questions, or it may be that the context of the interview inhibits a person from giving the correct response. The question may also *embarrass* the respondent because of the topic, e.g., a very intimate topic that the respondent would not normally discuss with a stranger. In some cases, the respondent may see a *threat* in the question, for example if a question concerning income could have relation to tax returns. In an authoritarian society where religious and personal freedom is curtailed, it may seem to be too big a risk to answer a certain question.

The best way to solve such problems is to have *anonymous* questionnaires where the identity of the respondent cannot be traced. This is fairly simple with mail interviews. In a personal interview confidentiality can be promised but not necessarily believed. The respondent will therefore need to be convinced of the necessity of the question. Indirect questions such as, "What would people in this community respond to . . . ?" is more likely to gain an accurate response than a direct, personal question.

Research Purpose	Questions designed to obtain the information
Research Objective #1	
Information Need 1.1	Questions number
Information Need 1.2	Questions number
Information Need 1.3	Questions number
Information Need 1.4	Questions number
Information Need 1.5	Questions number
Research Objective #2	
Information Need 2.1	Questions number
Information Need 2.2	Questions number

Figure 8. 3
Relationship of Questions to Information Needs

Question Content

There should be a logical flow from information needs to questions on a questionnaire. The question content will seek to obtain the information from the respondents as called for by the Information Needs.

In order to keep a careful check on the need for certain questions, it is helpful to have a checklist as the one suggested in chapter 5 and briefly illustrated in figure 8.3.

Response Format

After considering question content, the next issue concerns the type of questions to be asked and the corresponding response format. The degree of sophistication in question structure varies from completely unstructured to highly structured questions. Generally speaking, the structured formats help with coding and data tabulation as they can be prepared for direct computer entry. In this chapter we will deal with simple types of questions, and the following chapter will consider more sophisticated rating scales.

Open-ended questions require respondents to formulate and provide their own answers to the questions given. In a personal interview the interviewer will write down the response as it is given, and on a mail questionnaire, a blank space is provided for the respondent to fill in. This approach may look appealing and tempting and it has its advantages.

Open-ended questions allow general attitudes to be expressed, and this may be good as the opening question in a personal interview. The responses will be less influenced by the question than in a multi-choice question where a predetermined set of responses are provided. Alternatives can be freely expressed, and this makes open-ended questions especially useful in exploratory research. The answers may also provide an extra dimension to the feelings of the respondent.

But there are serious disadvantages with open-ended questions. There are possibilities for interviewer bias as the answers may not be recorded exactly as stated, or may be summarized in the interviewer's words. Another disadvantage is the cost and time involved in coding the responses, and especially in large surveys this can be a significant part of the whole budget. This can be partly overcome by providing a list of pre-coded responses from which the interviewer selects the appropriate response alternative after listening to the respondent's reply.

Open-ended questions also tend to give more weight to the most articulate respondents who are able to formulate responses. On self-administered questionnaires people tend to write brief responses, giving problems of interpretation, and their handwriting may be illegible.

With these limitations in mind, it will be well to keep open-ended questions primarily for exploratory research, and then spend the necessary time to develop other types of questions for the actual questionnaire.

Multi-choice questions require a person to select an answer from among a given set of alternatives. Multi-choice questions overcome most of the problems raised above for open-ended questions.

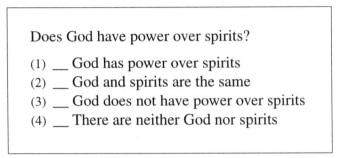

Does God have power over spirits?

(1) __ God has power over spirits
(2) __ God and spirits are the same
(3) __ God does not have power over spirits
(4) __ There are neither God nor spirits

Figure 8. 4
Multi-choice Question

Interviewer bias, time, and coding cost are all significantly reduced with multi-choice questions. For self-administered questionnaires, it is also easier to obtain and keep the cooperation of the respondent when multi-choice questions are used.

The disadvantage of multi-choice questions is that extensive time and work is involved in developing the questions. Often exploratory research needs to be carried out for this purpose so that the right alternative answers can be obtained. If significant alternatives are left out, the responses may be substantially biased, and there may also be position bias due to the order of the alternatives given.

The illustration in figure 8.5 is from a recent research in an African country which was aimed at identifying people's cognitive, affective, and behavioral positions in relation to a set of key theological terms.[2] As the alternative answers were aiming at positioning the respondents in a certain process, the order of the responses was scrambled as shown on the following illustration. Obviously, the scrambling codes given on the left

2. Research conducted by James Kantiok as part of doctoral studies at Fuller Seminary School of World Mission, California. 1995-96.

side in figure 8.5 were not provided on the questionnaires themselves. At the time of data entry, the entries were made according to the given codes.

---

10. How do you understand the Scriptures?

2 ☐ (1) The Quran has more authority than the Bible
3 ☐ (2) The Bible has more authority than the Quran
4 ☐ (3) The Bible is the final Scripture
1 ☐ (4) The Quran is the final Scripture

11. What is your feeling about the Scriptures?

3 ☐ (1) I am blessed more by the Bible than by the Quran
4 ☐ (2) My greatest blessing is through the Bible
1 ☐ (3) My greatest blessing is through the Quran
2 ☐ (4) I am blessed more by the Quran than by the Bible

Figure 8. 5

Illustration of Multi-Choice Questions Where Response Order Is Scrambled to Avoid Guessing on Behalf the Respondent.

There are two basic considerations for multi-choice questions: (1) alternatives must be collectively exhaustive, that is, all possible responses must be included. (2) Alternative responses must be mutually exclusive, that is, a respondent must be able to identify only one response. There are situations, though, when the respondent is asked to make more than one choice.

On a mail questionnaire, it is easy to list the alternatives, and in a personal interview, alternative responses may be provided on a card for the respondent. For a telephone interview, the list of alternatives must of course be short and easy to remember. In order to avoid position bias, the order of alternatives will usually be scrambled.

| Was the service good | __ yes __ no |
| Was the program to your satisfaction | __ yes __ no |

Figure 8. 6
Illustration of Dichotomous Questions Which
Do Not Provide Helpful Information

	Yes	Not Really
1. I can tell of a specific answer to prayer within the past month.	☐	☐
2. I take time for personal Bible reading at least three times a week.	☐	☐
3. Praying together as a family is part of our home life.	☐	☐
4. God's presence is real to me during group worship services in my church.	☐	☐
5. I am meaningfully involved in the life of our church through use of my spiritual gifts.	☐	☐
6. There is a positive spirit of oneness in our congregation.	☐	☐
7. Within the past two months I have invited a non-Christian into my home to visit.	☐	☐
8. I am proud enough of our church that I feel free to recommend it to my closes friends and neighbors.	☐	☐

Figure 8. 7
Good Alternative to Dichotomous Questions

Dichotomous questions, or **Yes-No** questions, allow the respondent only two possible answers, yes or no, agree or disagree, and so on. The advantages are easy pre-coding and easy to administer, saving time for the respondent. But there are also disadvantages, especially if it is wrongly assumed that only dichotomous answers are possible. This will create measurement error. In many situations a graded answer would be more acceptable, or at least has provision for a neutral response. The illustration in figure 8.6 clearly identifies the problem. The questionnaire was handed to patrons in a restaurant after they had participated in a large buffet lunch, and where nobody would be able to answer no to any of the questions.

Forcing a positive or negative answer may give the wrong impression. On the other hand, if a neutral response is possible, the person may select that even though he or she does not have a neutral position in relation to the question. If very few select the neutral position in a pretest, it may be advisable to force a yes or no position on the survey form.

A helpful way of solving the obstacles to a dichotomous question is to use the terms *yes/not really* as in the illustration in figure 8.7. *Not really* means *no*, but it is easier to respond that way. The illustration has been adapted from a questionnaire by Indepth Evangelism Associates.[3]

Phrasing the Question

As mentioned earlier, the questions on a questionnaire form the direct link between the information needs and the source of the data. The formulation of the questions is a very sensitive matter, and cultural values will often dictate how questions are asked. There are no universal guidelines for how the questions should be phrased, but the following points are provided on the basis of experience by various researchers. It is of utmost importance that the researcher and the person answering the questions attach the same meaning to the questions. Only through pretesting is it possible to assure that this is the case.

Is the language appropriate for the respondent? The questions need to be consistent with the vocabulary level of the respondent, but generally speaking we should always aim for simplicity and use clear words. Test the vocabulary skills of the research population so that the respondent will not be either intimidated or feel talked down to.

Religious words often carry different connotations, even among different Christian groups. When researching among other religions, we may find that the same words are used, but with different meanings attached.

---

3. Indepth Evangelism Associates is a ministry of the Latin American Mission.

Are the words ambiguous? Many words are ambiguous and do not provide accurate information. Be aware of such words as "usually," "regularly," and "frequently." For some it may mean attending church once a week, for others once a year. We also need to consult a dictionary to see if a word has more than one meaning, or if it can be pronounced in more than one way. As a general rule, *if a question can be misunderstood, it is not good enough.*

Is it a leading question? A leading question is a question where the respondent is given a cue, consciously or unconsciously, as to what answer the researcher would like to have. Such questions will give constant measurement error in the results.

It has often been found that many people will tend to select an answer that they think the interviewer is looking for. For example, if a researcher from the Christian radio station DZAS in Manila asks the question, "Do you listen to radio station DZAS?" he or she would most likely get a much higher positive response and listenership than if the person was just asked, "Which radio stations do you listen to?"

Is the question biased? A biased question will include emotionally colored phrases or words that suggest a feeling of approval or disapproval. The bias can be caused by associating a response with a well-known personality or cause. For example, a question that would begin with the words, "Do you agree with Billy Graham that . . ." would most likely lead to a biased response. Such bias may, of course, be directed both for and against a person or topic. Response to biased questions may also change from group to group. In one group the mentioning of a prestigious person or organization may be a positive, in another group a negative. The only way to eliminate bias is to conduct extensive pretesting.

Are there implicit alternatives? Implicit alternatives may lead to useless information, as the respondent will try to guess what the alternatives are. On the other hand, responses to explicit alternatives may be influenced by the order of the response. Rating scales such as the semantic differential scale, which will be discussed later, will therefore need to have positive and negative traits alternated.

Do any of the questions build on implicit assumptions? The respondent may not know or have the information on which the question is based. For example, Christians often mistakenly assume that adherents of other religions actually are familiar with the teachings of such religions which is often not the case.

Are estimates avoided or clarified? An estimate is where a respondent is asked to provide a generalization which they are not necessarily able to provide. Requests for estimates should therefore be as clear as possible with specific alternatives given. The illustration given in figure 8.8 shows a question where the respondent's background will severely influence his or her response. A person coming from a church with significant growth may look at a new situation and judge it "slow growth," while a person from a background of no growth may judge it as "rapid growth."

What is the growth rate of the total Christian community among
    this people group?
    __ Rapid growth
    __ Slow growth
    __ Stable
    __ Slow decline
    __ Rapid decline

Figure 8. 8
Estimates without Any Frame of Reference
Can Give Very Misleading Answers

Is the question double-barreled? A double-barreled question is a question where two different sets of information is requested, that is, two questions in one. The word "and" in a question will often signify a double-barreled questions.

Has the New Testament been translated into this language and who reads it?

Figure 8. 9
Two Questions in One Will Confuse the Respondent

Is the questionnaire the correct length? It is impossible to give exact guidance on the length of a questionnaire as it depends on many factors. If the topic is of central interest to the respondent, he or she may be willing to cooperate during a long period of time, but we should be aware of fatigue. This can be tested during pretests. It also depends on time available, so a busy executive is less likely to fill out a long questionnaire in a hotel room than a retired couple on a long holiday would be. The newness of research will also play a role. In some instances a two-hour session may be possible, at other times five minutes may seem too long.

no longer than necessary

Sequence of Questions

A questionnaire needs a certain amount of order, and there needs to be a natural flow of questions, especially as seen from the perspective of the respondent.

Following earlier suggestions that the interviewing process needs to be a pleasant communication event, it is important that the first question is interesting for the respondent and simple enough to guarantee full understanding. The questions need to sound reasonable for the respondent in the context of the introductions given. Good rapport needs to be established. Maybe a question requesting an attitude will be a good starter.

Uninteresting questions, questions that need more thinking, and potentially embarrassing questions should be left to later in the questionnaire. After initial rapport has been achieved, the respondent will be less likely to object to the more demanding questions.

Sequencing is also important where one question may influence the answer to subsequent questions. When several questions are needed, it is good to begin with general questions, then follow with more specific questions. This reduces sequencing bias.

nice pleasant + to worked out

Layout Characteristics

The layout and physical characteristics of a questionnaire may significantly influence response rate. This is in particular so for self-administered questionnaires, as the first impression, like in any communication situation, influences the response. If the questionnaire is appealing and nice, we are more ready to spend time on filling it out. A questionnaire in an Indian restaurant was formed as a greeting card with nice colors, providing a pleasant atmosphere for the response.

Figure 8. 10
Questionnaire Formed as a Greeting Card

Figures 8.11 and 8.12 give two examples of questionnaires presented to airline passengers just after a meal has been consumed. Figure 8.11 fits the atmosphere of a plane just after a meal when passengers want to relax. Figure 8.12 immediately turns you off and your feeling is that this questionnaire is for the engineer.

A questionnaire must be easy to fill out. The respondent needs to have the impression that the research organization has done everything they can to assist the respondent in cutting down the time needed to answer the questions. This also means that styles of response should be consistent through sections of the questionnaires. A special challenge is present when two different languages are to be used. Figures 8.13 and 8.14 provide good examples of how this was handled by two airlines.

Questions on a questionnaire should all be precoded and ready for direct input into a computer. Each item of information therefore needs its own number, ideally corresponding directly with the number of the data field in the computer.

Figure 8. 11
A Questionnaire Cover That Gives You a Feeling of Relaxation
(a free pen was provided)

AIRLINES

Dear Passenger:

United Airlines is pleased you have chosen to fly with us today. In order to provide you with the best possible travel experience, we would like to know a little more about you and why you are traveling today. You can help us by taking a few moments to complete this questionnaire. Your flight attendant will collect the completed forms.

Thank you for your assistance.

James E. Goodwin
Senior Vice President, Marketing

DIRECTIONS: This form is processed by machine. PLEASE read and follow these instructions:

A. Use pencil (do not use ink).*
B. Erase errors completely.
C. Avoid making stray marks.
D. Place comments in space at end of survey.

EXAMPLE — PROPER MARKS — IMPROPER MARKS

*If you do not have a pencil, your flight attendant will provide one.

THE QUESTIONS BELOW PERTAIN TO THE TRAVEL PLANS AND EXPERIENCES FOR THE FLIGHT YOU ARE ON RIGHT NOW. PLEASE THINK ABOUT THIS PARTICULAR FLIGHT WHEN ANSWERING THE FOLLOWING QUESTIONS:

1a. What is your flight number?

1b. Today's date:

1c. In what city did you board this flight?

2. How close to the scheduled departure time did this flight leave the gate?
- O On time
- O 1-5 minutes late
- O 6-15 minutes late
- O 16-30 minutes late
- O 31-60 minutes late
- O Over 60 minutes late

3. Where are you seated on today's flight?
- a. Cabin: O First Class O Business O Coach
- b. Section: O Smoking O Non-Smoking
- c. Seat: O Window O Aisle O Other

4. Printed below is a sample of a typical ticket (yours may vary slightly). Locate your ticket number in the upper right corner of your ticket or voucher (as illustrated). Please copy THE LAST 6 DIGITS of your ticket or voucher number in the appropriate spaces provided and fill in the matching circles below each number, as shown in the example below. The ticket number will provide information about your exact fare and itinerary but will not reveal your identity.

EXAMPLE

0 9 0 3 6 5

Fill matching circles below

SAMPLE TICKET

016 4452 123456

DATE AND PLACE OF ISSUE

COPY: Last 6 digits of your Ticket No. here

Fill matching circles below

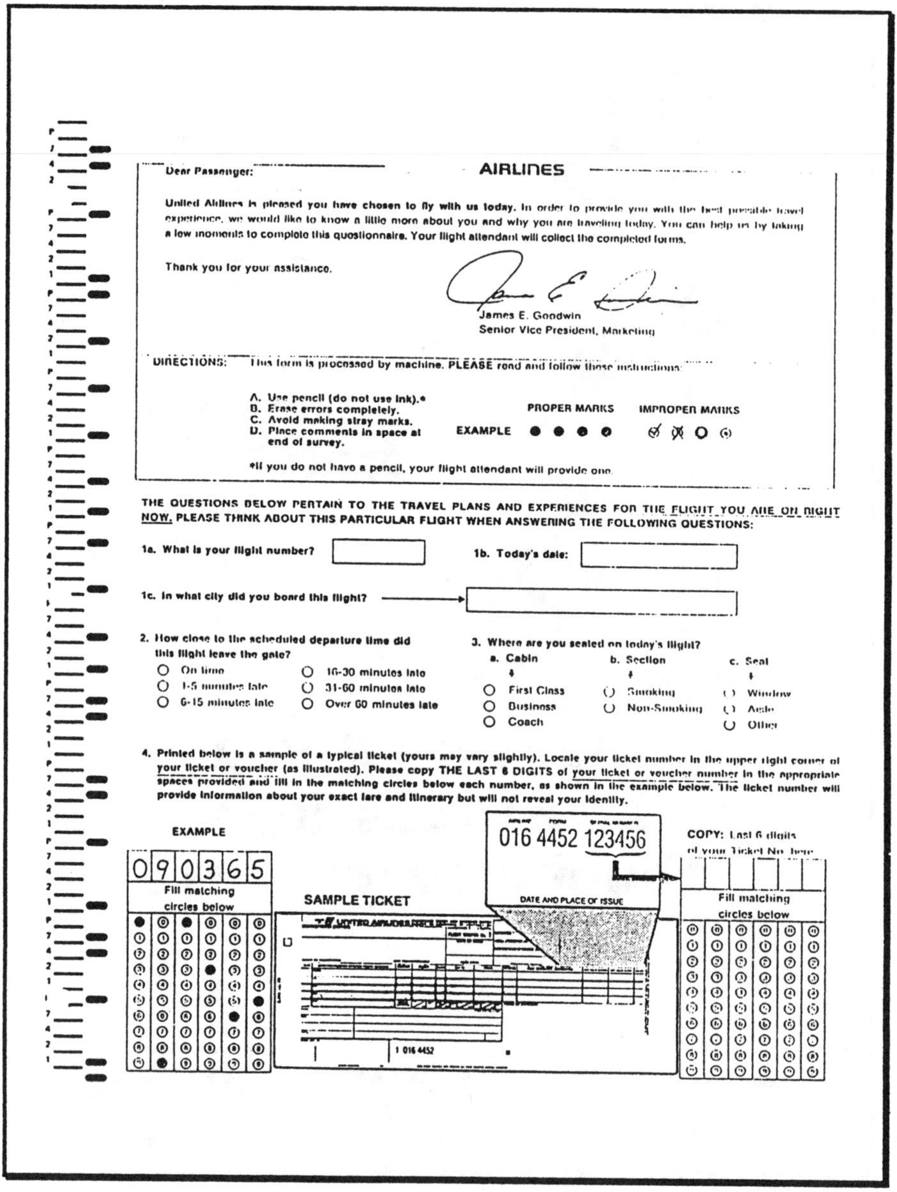

Figure 8. 12

A Questionnaire Cover That Makes You Call the Engineer!

	ناقص UNSATIS-FACTORY	مناسب SATIS-FACTORY	اعلیٰ EXCE-LLENT		
Dear Passenger,				**Reservation/Ticketing**	ریزرویشن/ٹکٹنگ
It has always been our endeavour to make your flight with us as pleasant as possible. We are however conscious of the fact that there is always room for improvement.	☐	☐	☐	Convenience in obtaining booking	نشست کے حصول میں آسانی
	☐	☐	☐	Service	عملہ کی خدمات
We attach considerable importance to the opinion of our passengers on all aspects of our service. Therefore you are requested to fill up this questionnaire by placing a tick ✓ in the appropriate box. Fold the form and hand it over to the flight attendants or post it to us, your views will help us make further improvements.	☐	☐	☐	Courtesy	عملہ کا رویہ
				Check-In	چیک اِن
	☐	☐	☐	Service	عملہ کی خدمات
	☐	☐	☐	Courtesy	عملہ کا رویہ
Thank you for your co-operation.				**Departure Lounge**	روانگی لاؤنج
Managing Director	☐	☐	☐	Staff Assistance	عملہ کی خدمات
	☐	☐	☐	Announcements	اعلانات
				Inflight Service	دورانِ پرواز کارکردگی
	☐	☐	☐	Service	عملہ کی خدمات
	☐	☐	☐	Courtesy	عملہ کا رویہ
				Inflight Announcements	دوران پرواز اعلانات
	☐	☐	☐	P.A. System Functioning	آواز کی جماعت کا نظام
	☐	☐	☐	Quality	معیار
Cher Passager,				**Food**	کھانا
Nous nous sommes toujours efforces de rendre votre voyage sur notre compagnie le plus agréable possible. Nous attachons beaucoup d'importance à l'opinion de nos passagers sur tous les aspects de notre service. Pour cela, nous vous prions de bien vouloir remplir ce questionnaire en cochant les cases appropriées. Remplissez ce formulaire et remettez le aux employés de notre compagnie ou envoyez nous le. Votre point de vue peut nous aider à realiser dans le futur des ameliorations.	☐	☐	☐	Quality	معیار
	☐	☐	☐	Presentation	خوبصورتی
				Aircraft Cabin	جہاز کی اندرونی حالت
	☐	☐	☐	Cabin Appearance/Cleanliness	کیبن کی حالت/صفائی
	☐	☐	☐	Seat Reclining Mechanism	نشست کو آرام دہ کرنے کا نظام
				Toilets	بیت الخلا
Merci de votre cooperation.					
Le Directeur General	☐	☐	☐	Fixtures	تنصیبات
	☐	☐	☐	Cleanliness	صفائی
C 搭乗の皆様へ	☐	☐	☐	Amenities	فروری کی اشیاء کی فراہمی
私共は常にお客様が快適に C 飛行できるよう努力いたしております が、更によりよいサービスをめざし てお客様の C 産場を率にさせていただ きたいと考えております。 つきましては、今社のサービスについてお気付きの点が C ざいましたら本カードの該当欄に記入のうえ、折りたたんで C 搭乗乗務員にお渡しいただくか、C 郵送ください。 C 協力ありがとうございました。				**Transit/Transfer Service**	ٹرانزٹ/ٹرانسفر خدمات
	☐	☐	☐	Promptness	بروقتگی
	☐	☐	☐	Staff Assistance	عملہ کا تعاون
				Inflight Entertainment *	تفریحی سہولیات
	☐	☐	☐	Seat Music - Choice	نشست، موسیقی، انتخاب
取締役社長	☐	☐	☐	Quality	معیار
	☐	☐	☐	Movies - Choice Projection	فلم، انتخاب، پراجیکشن
	☐	☐	☐	Sound	آواز

Form No. 9-30-170

* On International Routes only — مرف بین الاقوامی پروازوں پر

Figure 8. 13
Illustration of Questionnaire with Four-Language
Introduction and Two Language Questions

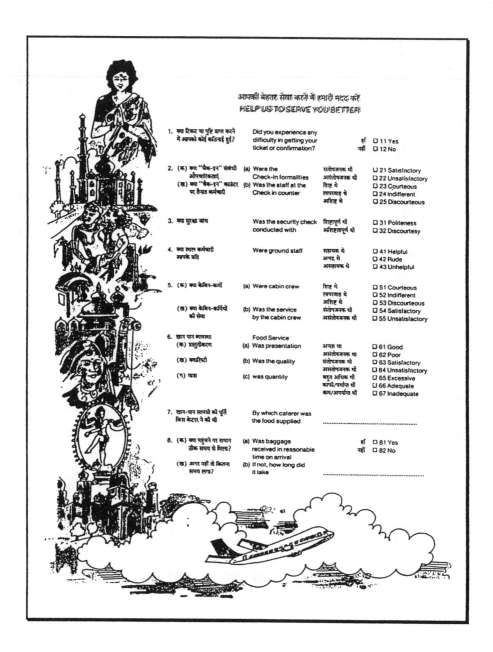

Figure 8. 14
Questionnaire with Two Languages and Ample Illustrations

CHECKLIST FOR QUESTIONNAIRE

Based on personal experiences with research projects, the checklist presented in figure 8.15 has been compiled. Each of these questions should be asked concerning each question on a questionnaire.

---

1. *Is the question necessary?*
2. *Are several questions needed instead of just one?*
3. *Does the respondent have the information?*
4. *Does the respondent have any experience with the subject?*
5. *Does the respondent remember the necessary information?*
6. *Is the respondent willing to give the required information?*
7. *Does the question look reasonable to the respondent?*
8. *Is the question ambiguous?*
9. *Is the question biased?*
10. *Is the question clear?*
11. *Is the question too broad?*
12. *Are you able to answer yes or no?*
13. *Do you need a graded answer?*
14. *Will the question(s) obtain the needed information?*
15. *Does the question embarrass the respondent?*
16. *Does the question frighten the respondent?*
17. *Are the questions in a logical order on the questionnaire?*
18. *Does any question influence the following questions?*
19. *Is the first question interesting to the respondent?*
20. *Does the questionnaire look interesting?*
21. *Is the questionnaire easy to use?*
22. *Has the questionnaire and the questions been pretested?*

Figure 8. 15
Checklist for Questionnaires

Hello,
I am Buddy Budget.
May I ask you
something?

As a spokesman of the XXX Budget Hotel I kindly request you to answer a few questions, to enable the hotel management to use your opinion for improvements of service and quality. When answering, please keep in mind that the XXX Budget Hotel wishes to offer you the highest possible standard in connection with low budget rates.

Figure 8. 16
A Humorous Approach to Questionnaire Cover Page

9

RATING SCALES

Design Sampling Plan
Construct Data Collection Form
Data Collection in the Field

This chapter will continue the treatment of questionnaire construction, and it will add more advanced types of measurements and rating scales.

As we look at different parts of our environment and daily experiences, we need different kinds of special tools and techniques for gathering information about them. Some instruments, like a thermometer, can be used by anybody, but other instruments and techniques need training and practice if they are to be useful. For an untrained person a look into a microscope or telescope will tell him almost nothing. For others, numbers or economic data will make no sense. The novice needs to acquire a conceptual framework and gain additional experience before he or she can make appropriate interpretation of the data. Likewise, the communication researcher must, in addition to the basic tools and instruments of observation and measurement, have a general conceptual framework for sorting out and organizing the data received.

It is important for us to master both methodologies and techniques to obtain the reliable and valid information we need. A broadcaster cannot, for example, base the information-gathering solely on letters received from the audience, whether praising or complaining, as it is very difficult to tell how much of the audience they represent. Letters are important to many mass media programs, but the more experienced the mass communicators are, the more cautious they will be of unsystematic feedback.

RESEARCH MEASUREMENTS

Measurement is a fundamental aspect of research, and it is often stated that the best way to really understand something is to try to measure it. The measurement process involves using numbers to represent the phenomena under investigation, or we could say that measurement is concerned with developing a correspondence between the empirical system and the abstract system.[1]

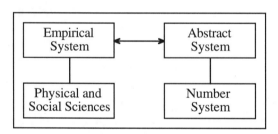

Figure 9. 1
The Measurement Process

When developing an abstract system for measurement, numbers will then have to be assigned to characteristics of objects or events according certain established rules. The closer the relationship there is between the events in the empirical system and the rules of the number system, the more accurate the data will be, and the less measurement error has occurred.

---

1. Adapted from Kinnear, Thomas C. and James R. Taylor, *Marketing Research, An Applied Approach*, 4rth ed. New York: McGraw-Hill Book Company, 1991:221.

It is also important to note that we are measuring characteristics of people or events, and not the people or events themselves. We do not, for example, measure the height and weight of a person, but his or her preference for a church or level of Bible knowledge.

Numbers are in themselves symbols used to indicate relations in a numbering system. Both the characteristics of the empirical system and the numbering system need to be taken into account.

The four characteristics of our numbering system are shown in figure 9.2, and in the use of statistics one or more of these characteristics are being used:

Each number in the series is unique
    (0, 1, 2, 3, 4, 5, 6, 7, 8, 9)

Ordering of numbers is given by convention
    (7 > 6, 2 > 1, i.e., 7 is more than 6, 2 is more than 1)

Equal differences can be defined
    (8 - 6 = 5 - 3)

Equal ratios can be defined
    (10÷5 = 6÷3)

Figure 9. 2
Characteristics of Our Numbering System

When some of these characteristics exist in the empirical system, we can select the appropriate statistic. The temptation is to use more characteristics of the numbering system than actually exist in the phenomena we are researching. Our manipulation of numbers and the use of statistics will need to be determined by how many of the above characteristics actually exist.

TYPES OF MEASUREMENT SCALES

Scales are classified in terms of the characteristics of the number system explained above. We have then:

- Nominal scales
- Ordinal scales
- Interval scales
- Ratio scales

For each of these scales there are special statistical formulas available as indicated on the chart in figure 9.3. Statistics appropriate for nominal measurements are also appropriate for higher scales, and the same is true of ordinal and interval scales.

Nominal Scales   unique –

Nominal scales are used to assign numbers as labels. There are few restrictions as to how such numbers can be assigned and in themselves the numbers have no meaning or value. It can be the numbers given to football players. The only rule is that the same number can only be given once.

Nominal scales are then used for the lowest form of measurement, namely for classification and identification. A significant part of survey research requires the use of nominal scales as we need identification and classification data to study radio audiences, describe church membership, church attendance, involvement in ministry, etc. We need classification when comparing opinions of one group to that of another, for example, comparing the opinions of women to those of men.

Ordinal Scales

order of preference

Ordinal scales are used to place objects or events in some kind of order or relationship. It is to measure whether an object or an event has more or less of a characteristic than another object or event, but we cannot use this scale to indicate how much more or how much less. We can, for example, use the ordinal scale to indicate our preference for three different kinds of Bible translation. Which one we like best, which one is our second choice, and which one is third. It does not indicate how much more we like one in comparison to the other, though, or if the "distance" between one and two is the same as that between two and three.

The assignment of numbers in an ordinal scale is then more restricted than that of nominal scales. In ordinal scales we have a serial relationship so the ordered relationships of the empirical system must be safeguarded.

Scale	Number System	Permissible Statistics	Possible Uses
Nominal	Unique numbers (0, 1, 2, . . . 9)	Percentages Mode Chi-square test Binomial test	Male-female Members Denomination
Ordinal	Order of numbers (0<1<2<3 . . . <9)	Percentiles Median Rank-order correlation	Attitudes Preference Education
Interval	Equality of differences (8-1 = 5-4)	Range Mean Standard deviation	Attitudes Opinions
Ratio	Equality of ratios	Geometric mean Harmonic mean Coefficient of variation	Age Cost Number of members

Figure 9. 3
Types of Data and Examples of Statistics That Can Be Used[2]

It may be important to note that the appropriate statistic for measuring central tendency (averages) for ordinal data will be the median and not the mean, as the mean requires equal intervals. Much of our research will involve ordinal data, as we often need to study attitudes, preferences, and opinions where we ask for "greater than" or "less than" judgments. We will often need to rank such responses.

Interval Scales

On an interval scale the distance between the numerals will correspond to the distance between objects or events being measured. The unit of measurement has been arbitrarily determined and so has a zero point. One of

2. Adapted from Kinnear, Thomas C. and James R. Taylor, *Marketing Research, An Applied Approach*, 4th ed. New York: McGraw-Hill Book Company, 1991:223.

the most common uses of such interval scales is for the measurement of temperature. Fahrenheit and Celsius both measure temperature, but they use different numbers and different units of measurement. But as the zero point is arbitrarily assigned, you cannot say that 80° centigrade is double as hot as 40° centigrade, or that 122° F is double as hot as 61° F. The absence of an absolute zero point limits the choices for appropriate statistics.

Ratio Scales

Apart from having all the properties of the interval scale, the ratio scale also has an absolute zero point. The unit of measurement or distance may be assigned arbitrarily, but then all other numbers must follow the same system. We do have one measurement of temperature where a ratio scale is used and that is the Kelvin scale where the zero point represents the absolute absence of heat (-273.15° C). We can also use ratio for age, stating that a person of 36 years is twice as old as one who is 18 years old. Ratio scales can be used for money, stating that the offering this week is three times higher than last week, or we can talk of doubling the membership, etc. The entire range of statistical techniques can be applied to data obtained by ratio scales.

Numbers, Knowledge	Preferences, Attitudes	Happiness, Creativity
Easy to measure		Very difficult to measure

Figure 9. 4
Difficulty of Measurements

DIFFICULTIES OF MEASUREMENTS

Unfortunately, the measurement task in communication research is typically more difficult than the counting of numbers, as we know from church growth studies. The problem lies in the measurement of the behavior of people, and of measuring concepts believed to exist in people's minds. There are, of course, certain types of data that can be obtained relatively easily by counting, for example, conversions or the number of people listening to a sermon, but the majority of our studies will need to be based on increasingly difficult scales. Issues of faith are in the area which is very difficult to measure.

Constructs

Much of the data collected through survey research involves ordinal measurements, that is, putting products or concepts in some kind of order. It is the measurement of attitudes, opinions, preferences, and perceptions. Before we can study such opinions, they need to be defined. Often the characteristics cannot be observed directly, and consequently we need to define such constructs as precisely as possible. For example, we need measurable definitions if we are to study such topics as a person's loyalty to the family or to his or her church.

So, in order to measure constructs, we need to develop operational definitions that specify how a construct is to be measured, that is, provide the researcher with details of what he or she must do to measure it. For example, what are the observable or measurable characteristics of faith? We often hear statements such as, "He is a good Christian." But, do we measure that? What are the assumptions for such a statement? How do we infer the results from observable behavior or responses to questions?

Example of Shalom Measures

In one particular research project we were trying to measure holistic changes in people's lives, that is, changes seen in the perspective of the Kingdom of God. This particular case study will be reported more completely in chapter 14, but let us look briefly at how definitions were established.

The objectives called for measurements covering the areas of relationship to God, to self, to others, to creation, and to the church. This would then include topics related to theology, psychology, sociology, ecology,

Shelow destroyed at the Fall —

and ecclesiology. The first step was to define a standard for what the right relationships were in these areas and then to arrive at selected indicators from which we would be able to infer the results. This activity was what we can call the definition of constructs.

Following the development of standards and indicators, it was possible to develop appropriate process measures for each area. The research was done in cognitive, affective, and behavioral categories, that is, what the respondents know, how they feel, and how they act in relation to the topic.

VALID AND RELIABLE RESEARCH FINDINGS

Careful attention to possible *measurement error* will help us gather valid, reliable, and useful data. Good definitions of constructs will help considerably as we attempt to find correspondence between a numbering system and the phenomena being measured.

There are several areas where error can easily creep in:[3]

1. *Characteristics measured and data obtained may be short-term, influenced by external factors such as mood and fatigue.*
2. *Characteristics measured and data obtained may be influenced by situational factors such as change in location.*
3. *Characteristics measured and data obtained may be influenced by the way questions are asked and the personality of interviewers.*
4. *Characteristics measured and data obtained may be inconsistent due to measuring factors such as ambiguous questions.*
5. *Characteristics measured and data obtained may be changed by coding and tabulation errors.*

The total error of measurement is a combination of systematic error and random error. Systematic error will be caused by a constant measuring error like the wrong speed of a stop-watch. Random error is where different stop-watches are used in a competition and one of them is not consistent.

For good research and help in the decision-making process, it is clear that we need reliable and valid information. Reliability deals with consis-

---

3. Ibid., p. 231.

tency and accuracy, and it will be increased as we reduce all possible areas of error in the measurement process.

Validity is concerned with the question, Are we measuring what we think we are measuring? Normally, validity is treated from four perspectives:

Construct Validity involves understanding the theoretical rationale underlying the obtained measurements. This calls for careful conceptualization and development of a theoretical framework for the research project as was described above. *valid information + reliable info*

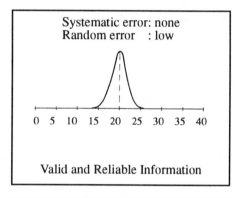

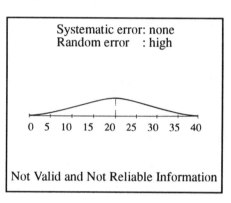

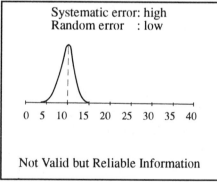

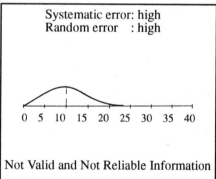

Figure 9. 5
Reliability and Validity

Content Validity involves a subjective judgment by an expert as to the appropriateness of the measurement. We may also call this "face validity" because of the emphasis on the expert's critical eye in determining the relevance of the measurements to the underlying construct. In a mission situation, it would be the evaluation done by a missionary with many years experience.

Concurrent Validity involves correlating two different measurements of the same phenomenon which have been administered at the same point in time. This approach may be especially useful when developing new measuring techniques, or when a translator is looking for a specific word for a new biblical concept.

Predictive Validity involves the ability to predict a future condition on the basis of a measured phenomenon. This may also involve repeated testing of the same person or group. There may also be two different questions aimed at obtaining the same information and the data is then compared. We should always be suspicious of results that are dramatically different from earlier results.

MEASUREMENT OF ATTITUDES

A discussion among a group of Christians may include the following statements:

I like the morning service. It gives me a good feeling.
There is a good fellowship in our church.
This new version of the Bible speaks to me.

Each of these attitudes are difficult to define in measurable terms, but they are obviously important if good communication strategies are to be worked out. Attitudes are also important because of the assumed relationship between attitudes and behavior. Attitudinal data is used to identify audience segments and to measure openness to change. The Christian communicator needs, for example, to understand people's attitudes toward Christ and toward the church in order to prepare programs that are relevant and that will gain a listening.

Attitudes are usually understood to have three main components or dimensions: *cognitive* (awareness and knowledge), *affective* (feelings and likeness), and *behavioral* (intention to act or actual action).

By studying the cognitive and affective dimensions, we may, at least in some situations, be able to predict a behavioral change. A combination of knowledge and feelings is usually assumed to determine the intention to act. But there are many other factors that also influence the final decision to act or not to act. There may be financial or social constraints. In Muslim societies the constraints placed on younger members of the family may cause some to avoid taking behavioral steps in response to their faith, and in some countries the social pressure from the family may make it next to impossible for girls to make individual decisions.

Attitudes are usually measured by nominal or ordinal scales of measurement, and it will focus on a person's beliefs or knowledge about a topic or object, and his or her feelings towards that same topic or object. This can be understanding (or misunderstanding) of Christianity and feelings towards Christianity. In the introduction to this book, an example was given of a research study in which people were measured regarding their responses to the terms Christ and Christian. Only when there was a change in attitude did behavioral changes take place. So, a positive attitude is normally required before behavioral steps can be expected. We have seen, though, that where there are people movements towards Christ, the affective and behavioral dimensions may be well ahead of changes in the cognitive dimension.

A number of different techniques can be used for measuring attitudes, ranging from self-reports to observations. The simplest form is a nominal scale where a respondent's knowledge or beliefs are classified into two or more categories. This may be "yes" or "no," and possibly a third category "don't know." Numbers assigned to such categories will serve as identification only.

Usually graded answers are needed for affective measures, called rating scales. On such a scale, the respondent is asked to indicate a position on a continuum, from liking to disliking, or from agree to disagree. This can be further expanded to a system where the respondents are asked to choose one sentence among four alternatives to indicate their own feelings or beliefs about a given subject.

Rating scales can also be given verbally, but then the number of categories has to be small enough to easily identify the alternatives. It may also consist of a number of statements and the respondent chooses the alternative that is closest to his or her preference, or it may be a series of comparisons. The illustration given in figure 9.6 is from an African country, and the study was conducted among non-literate people. The question and the alternatives were read three times to each person. The first time they were asked to just listen to the question. The second time they should understand the question and prepare a response. The third time they actually gave their answer.

---

4. How is a person forgiven for his or her sins?

    ☐ (1) God will forgive if we offer sacrifice to him
    ☐ (2) God considers our obedience and forgives us
    ☐ (3) God forgives because of his mercy alone
    ☐ (4) God forgives if a person has faith in Jesus

Figure 9. 6
Illustration of Response Format

On a *Rank-order scale* respondents are required to put a series of characteristics into a desired order, or to rate a series of objects or events into an order of preference. This could be a congregation deciding among possible candidates for the vacant pastoral position.

27. Here are some statements on the in-flight magazine. To which extent do you agree or disagree on these statements? *attitude questions*

The magazine:	Quite agree	Agree to some extent	Neither agree nor dis- agree	Disagree to some extent	Quite disagree	
is informative	☐ 1	☐ 2	☐ 3	☐ 4	☐ 5	63
is entertaining	☐ 1	☐ 2	☐ 3	☐ 4	☐ 5	64
has interesting articles	☐ 1	☐ 2	☐ 3	☐ 4	☐ 5	65
is business oriented	☐ 1	☐ 2	☐ 3	☐ 4	☐ 5	66
is tourist oriented	☐ 1	☐ 2	☐ 3	☐ 4	☐ 5	67
has high quality lay-out	☐ 1	☐ 2	☐ 3	☐ 4	☐ 5	68
has high quality pictures	☐ 1	☐ 2	☐ 3	☐ 4	☐ 5	69
has interesting advertisements	☐ 1	☐ 2	☐ 3	☐ 4	☐ 5	70

Figure 9. 7
Part of Airline Questionnaire Illustrating Graded Answering
Format. All Questions and Answers Are Pre-Coded.

The *Semantic Differential Scale* is popular as an attitude measurement technique, and it can be used readily to add another dimension to our understanding of a person's attitudes. We can measure the image of an object or a person this way. Typically, a semantic differential scale has a seven point-rating scale between paired, but opposite words. Such scales are usually constructed for each specific application.

		Very much	Much	Some	Nei-ther	Some	Much	Very Much	
52.	Worth looking up to	☐	☐	☐	☐	☐	☐	☐	Not worth looking up to
53.	Fool	☐	☐	☐	☐	☐	☐	☐	Clever
54.	Important	☐	☐	☐	☐	☐	☐	☐	Not important
55.	Useful	☐	☐	☐	☐	☐	☐	☐	Useless
56.	Sell nation	☐	☐	☐	☐	☐	☐	☐	Love nation
57.	Enduring	☐	☐	☐	☐	☐	☐	☐	Not enduring
58.	Love neighbors	☐	☐	☐	☐	☐	☐	☐	Hate neighbors
59.	Sad	☐	☐	☐	☐	☐	☐	☐	Happy
60.	Joyful	☐	☐	☐	☐	☐	☐	☐	Gloomy
61.	Poor	☐	☐	☐	☐	☐	☐	☐	Rich
62.	Good friends	☐	☐	☐	☐	☐	☐	☐	Poor friends
63.	Have many friends	☐	☐	☐	☐	☐	☐	☐	Lonesome
64.	Good	☐	☐	☐	☐	☐	☐	☐	Bad

Figure 9. 8
Semantic Differential Scale from a Bangkok Study

The research was, of course conducted in Thai language and the actual form looked like the illustration in figure 9.9.

			มากที่สุด 1	มาก 2	บ้าง 3	ปานกลาง 4	บ้าง 5	มาก 6	มากที่สุด 7	
๕๒.	น่านับถือ	38	26	25	108	171	14	6	12	ไม่น่านับถือ
๕๓.	โง่	48	12	12	43	172	55	33	25	ฉลาด
๕๔.	สำคัญ	46	33	44	91	155	14	5	12	ไม่สำคัญ
๕๕.	เป็นประโยชน์	40	30	79	114	107	15	5	10	ไร้ประโยชน์
๕๖.	ขายชาติ	7	11	6	21	67	66	62	53	รักชาติ
๕๗.	มีความอดทน	54	63	97	51	103	8	10	14	ไม่มีความอดทน
๕๘.	รักเพื่อนบ้าน	62	45	80	75	115	12	5	6	เกลียดเพื่อนบ้าน
๕๙.	มีแต่ความทุกข์	65	12	12	38	111	67	62	33	มีความสุข
๖๐.	มีความร่าเริงใจ	59	42	70	80	120	14	4	11	มีแต่โศกเศร้า
๖๑.	ยากจน	65	14	6	35	199	35	31	15	ร่ำรวย
๖๒.	เป็นมิตรที่ดี	55	45	87	71	120	12	2	8	เป็นมิตรที่เลว
๖๓.	มีเพื่อนฝูงมาก	58	41	85	52	136	6	7	11	ว้าเหว่
๖๔.	ใจดี	55	49	80	61	135	11	1	8	"

Figure 9. 9
Part of Semantic Differential Scale in Thai
with Number of Responses Entered on the Form

A five-point scale would suffice on a semantic differential scale, but it has been found that people are reluctant to select the extreme positions, so expanding the scale to seven possible positions broadens the response. During actual tabulation, the two extreme positions on each side can usually be joined into one measure.

It has been argued that the semantic differential scale is not appropriate for non-Western cultures, but this viewpoint has been disproved in practice. The scale has been used successfully in both Asian and African settings. The argument has been that people tend to check the middle position, or the same position all the way through, but by providing good explanations and switching positive and negative dimensions from side to side, this can easily be overcome.

The *stapel scale* is a modification of the semantic differential scale. It provides one attribute and the respondent is asked to rate the object or event being studied on a +5 to -5 scale, or on a unipolar scale.

```
                              +5
                              +4
                              +3
                              +2
                              +1
              Friendly

                              -1
                              -2
                              -3
                              -4
                              -5
```

Figure 9. 10
Stapel Scale

The stapel scale can be used for measuring the comparative profiles of two or more organizations or churches.

```
Friendly    |__|__|__|__|__|__|__|__|__|
Honest      |__|__|__|__|__|__|__|__|__|
Convenient  |__|__|__|__|__|__|__|__|__|
Open        |__|__|__|__|__|__|__|__|__|
Warm        |__|__|__|__|__|__|__|__|__|
Concerned   |__|__|__|__|__|__|__|__|__|
Services    |__|__|__|__|__|__|__|__|__|
```

Figure 9. 11
Stapel Scale for Comparative Profiles

The *Likert Scale* is an indirect scale where a respondent is asked to indicate agreement or disagreement with a statement. The normal choices are:

☐ Strongly agree
☐ Agree
☐ Neither agree nor disagree
☐ Strongly disagree

Figure 9. 12
Response Format on Likert Scale

The scale can also be used as a graphic rating scale with faces, ranging from happy to sad.

After visiting our church, how do you feel about the experience?

1. Welcome on arrival at the church

2. Comfortable seats

3. Cleanliness of facilities

4. Decorations and atmosphere

5. Congregational singing

6. Warmth and fellowship

7. Relevancy of sermon

8. Overall impression of church

9. Recommend church to others

Figure 9. 13
Graphic Rating Scale

An adaptation of the Likert scale has been used in some studies. Instead of written responses boxes of different sizes were used: big, medium and small sizes. People are asked to indicate how much they personally identified with the position advocated by selecting the appropriate box. For example, the big box would be: "This is very much like me." A blank line can be added to indicate that "this is not like me."

Similar adaptation has been made of the +/- scale to have a four-point measure. It has been found helpful to use such an approach when trying to discover people's felt needs. The approach was used in a study where underlying mission principles were studied.

How much were the following principles or issues involved in this mission?	Not really (1)	Some (2)	Much (3)	Very much (4)
1. The Mission can be characterized as having a goal oriented approach				
2. The Mission utilized an incarnational model with people actually living among the group being reached				
3. The Mission used a person-based approach with focus on personal testimony and life of the evangelists				
4. The Mission was need-oriented and the approach focused on meeting specific needs of the audience				
5. The Mission used culturally relevant approaches with which the group was familiar				
6. The Mission focused on development of community (church) rather than on individual conversion				
7. The Mission emphasized the development of local leadership, training them and giving them authority				
8. The Mission emphasized the authority of the Scriptures, using the Word of God as final authority				
9. The Mission has a holistic ministry perspectives, meeting the needs of the total person				

Figure 9. 14
Part of Questionnaire Using Modified Likert Scale

Consistency

A questionnaire needs a certain amount of consistency, so only a few approaches or types of scales should be used on the same form. For mail questionnaires, it will often be necessary to provide explanations as to how a certain question should be answered when you change from one response format to another.

Pre-code

Every question have a unique #.
Consecutive #'s not sections + numbers

10

DATA COLLECTION

Field work
Interview Process

Construct Data Collection Form
Data Collection in the Field
Tabulation and Analysis of Data

Data collection in the field is the phase of the research project where interviewers meet the respondents, or self-administered questionnaires are filled out by selected people. The time spent in defining objectives and information needs, and the skills applied to questionnaire construction will be wasted if the data collection process is poorly carried out. In this chapter we will therefore deal with the actual (1) planning of data collection, (2) interviewer selection and training, (3) achieving cooperation from respondents, (4) asking questions, (5) recording responses, and (6) evaluation of obtained data.

PLANNING DATA COLLECTION

Several of the planning issues will possibly have been taken care of at an earlier stage in the research project, but a review will be important at this

169

point. First of all, a realistic time schedule will need to be worked out for data collection. In many countries around the world, lengthy delays may be experienced, and many external factors will demand time. Mail surveys will need to consider the actual time a letter may take to reach the respondent, time for a follow-up letter, and time for mail to get back. But for all surveys, the shorter the period can be, the more likely it is that the data will be consistent. A time schedule can be prepared on a flow diagram as illustrated in figure 10.1.

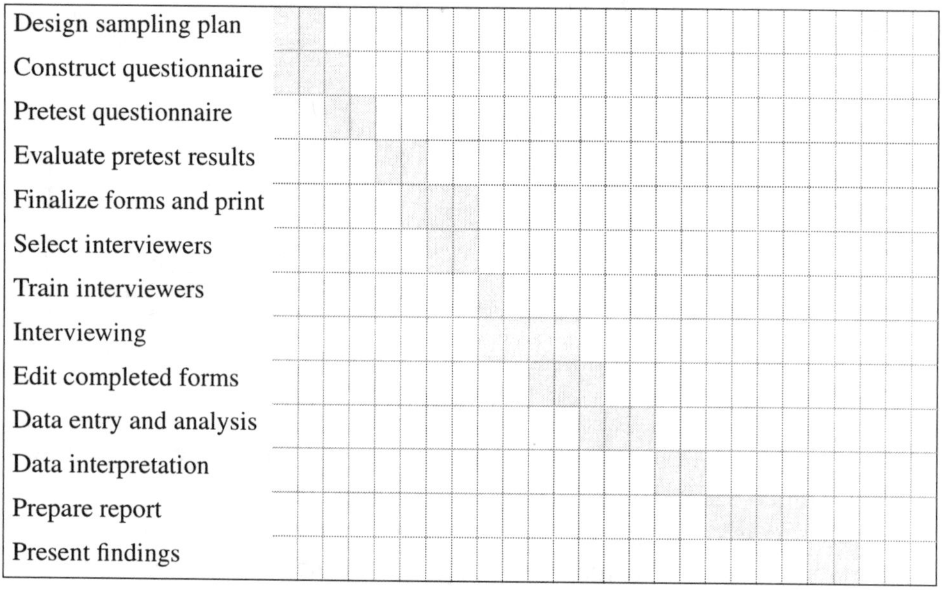

Design sampling plan
Construct questionnaire
Pretest questionnaire
Evaluate pretest results
Finalize forms and print
Select interviewers
Train interviewers
Interviewing
Edit completed forms
Data entry and analysis
Data interpretation
Prepare report
Present findings

Figure 10. 1
Time Schedule for Data Collection Process

BUDGET FOR DATA COLLECTION

The chart in figure 10.1 is given to illustrate the need for a planned process. Budgeting will probably have taken place at an earlier stage in the research process, but let us review it here. Many of the activities mentioned on the time-schedule above will demand a budget. Among the expenses will be:

- office expenses and secretarial help
- printing of questionnaires
- envelopes and postage for mail surveys
- cost of telephone for phone interviews
- salary for supervisor of interviewing process
- compensation for interviewers
- travel expenses for interviews
- computer facilities for data entry and tabulation
- analysis and reporting.

The size of the sample, the location of respondents, and the actual research design will all significantly influence the actual cost of these areas.

In Christian work, there will always be a question as to whether interviewers should be paid a honorarium or we should depend on volunteers. No clear-cut answer can be given to this question, but all interviews must be conducted at a professional level, and the less number of interviewers involved, the more accurate will be the results. If payment is given, it should be at a reasonable level, and it can be either as an hourly rate or payment for each completed interview. If payment is by the hour, the interviewer will not be tempted to finish the session in a rush and thus obtain questionable results. On the other hand, budgets will be easier to control when payment is given for each completed interview. In both cases, there should be some form of performance evaluation and control.

INTERVIEWER SELECTION

We need to select interviewers who in a given situation are most likely to obtain accurate responses. The selection should, therefore, focus on those whose background and appearance are compatible with those in the sample and who would gain their accept and trust. Students from a university will often be rejected or mistrusted by rural people, and a person of one race and color will rarely function well among a people of a different race and color. There will always be exceptions, but those who are chosen must be able to keep complete neutrality in the interviewing process and record data faithfully as given by the respondent.

Training of Interviewers

If professional or experienced interviewers are used, training may be limited to a brief session of instruction. But usually training will need to be an extended session of instruction where the following topics are covered:

- A thorough explanation of the research process
- Interviewers are made familiar with the questionnaire
- Training through role-plays where they interview each other
- Carry out a few actual interviews under supervision
- Information about practical details related to the research.

All instruction as to how to approach the respondent, how to establish rapport and get cooperation, and how to ask the questions will be provided in writing. Further training can then be provided as part of the supervised field work.

For a research project in rural Bangladesh, interviewers were trained to work in teams of two.[1] A senior man and a student would form a team. The senior man would gain acceptance and provide credibility for the interview, and the young man would assure that the interview was conducted as they were instructed. This proved to be an excellent approach for this particular cultural context.

Some surveys call for the use of interviewers in different countries so on-the-spot training is not possible. Careful instructions will then have to be given in writing. Experience shows that this is possible, but it will need extremely detailed instructions, and there is always the risk that some of the interviewers will disregard the instructions.

ACHIEVING COOPERATION TO CONDUCT THE INTERVIEW

A personal interview is an interpersonal communication situation and is therefore subject to all the principles of good communication. In a com-

---

1. An extensive research project was carried out in Bangladesh under the direction of Ms. Teresa Chai. The purpose was to develop a new approach to a Scripture-based literacy training program. Several tests were conducted in rural settings 1992–95. A complete research report is available through the United Bible Societies, 1996.

munity, it is also necessary to obtain the necessary permission from the leaders of the community. In some places, official permits are also required. Endorsement from known and respected officials or leaders will often be mandatory to achieve cooperation. This can be in the form of a letter from a church leader or from the pastor which has been sent to participants ahead of time, or it can be an official endorsement from a government office. For a survey conducted in schools, it was necessary to first obtain permission from the school principal, and then from the teacher concerned.[2] When that was achieved, there was no problem in getting students to be involved in the study.

Usually, we need to ask questions and receive responses from individual people, but at other times you need to test with a whole group. Very few people will refuse to help if you approach them nicely and ask them to help you. A nice-looking questionnaire that seems to be fairly easy to fill out will get a more positive reception than one that looks poorly done.

In some situations it may be difficult to gain access to the desired respondent. For example, this can be particularly troublesome in some Muslim countries if the respondent is a woman. Cultural norms do not readily bend to the researcher's wishes.

Getting cooperation on the phone is a little more sensitive as the respondent cannot see the interviewer. A brief statement of purpose and name of the research organization will often be all that can be done. In some situations, it is possible to give advance notification. This could be a church congregation who will be informed that they may get a call during the coming week. They will then be ready to cooperate and answer the questions.

Getting people to fill out a mailed questionnaire will also take careful planning. Advance notification is sometimes possible, but a cover letter from a respected person is usually the best. The questionnaire itself will also have introductions that aim at achieving cooperation. A self-addressed envelope for the response is important, and if possible it should be hand stamped. People will not throw a stamped envelope away, so this is a further inducement to complete the questionnaire. A value is also communicated by the fact that the researcher is willing to spend the extra

---

2. Viggo B. Søgaard, "Product Testing of Living Gospel of Mark in Thai." Unpublished research report, 1976.

money. In some instances it may also be possible to offer a small gift or token of appreciation as a further incentive to answer the questions.

Establish Rapport with the Respondent

The place where the interview is conducted is often very important. The interviewing guide prepared for the research study should stress the importance of privacy during the interview itself. In a village situation, the presence of an interviewer will attract a crowd, and many people will want to listen or look on, so often all you can do is strive for privacy but accept the circumstances as they arise. Then try to establish a good rapport with the respondent so that he or she does not feel inhibited by the social setting or context. Spend time talking with the person, especially if he or she is a stranger to you. The respondents need to trust you with their time and insights. Try to find a time that is convenient for the respondent so that the interview can be carried out in a relaxed atmosphere. The purpose of the study should be explained to the respondent so that he or she can see the value of giving you their time. Encouragement should be given for him or her to provide accurate responses.

In a phone interview, the interviewer will ask the respondent if this is a convenient time, but on the other hand he or she will do their best to complete the interview during the first call. A friendly voice will be important.

It is expected that the researcher has been made well aware of the audience and their situation. Are they able to read and write? Is the topic one that they are familiar with? Would certain illustrations be seen as threatening? Is the language or dialect of special importance?

Encourage Frank Responses

Through the research you are testing characteristics of people, programs and materials, not the people themselves. Therefore, point this out clearly to the respondent and explain that there are no correct answers. All we need are their frank responses. Resist the temptation to teach or preach, even if the answers seem to call for that. If teaching or preaching is mixed with the interview, your are not only breaking ethical rules regarding research, but you will most likely get a biased response.

The written questionnaire will need to have the necessary introduction to obtain frank responses, explaining that it is important that they give the exact information. If it is a long questionnaire, encouragement can be given at regular intervals.

ASKING QUESTIONS

It is always best to conduct an interview in a natural, conversational manner. But no changes whatsoever are permitted regarding phrasing of a question unless this has been stated in training as being allowable in specific instances. If wording varies from one interviewer to another, then the results are invalidated by random error.

Interviewers also should be aware that changes in voice intonation and gestures can be a source of bias. If a questionnaire has been well constructed, it should be without biased questions, but there is always a temptation or a tendency to ask the question in a leading voice. What would happen, for example, if voice stress were placed on the underlined words in this question?   *can bias the answer —*

During our Sunday morning service, do you prefer the <u>senior pastor</u> to preach or the associate pastor?

During our Sunday morning service, do you prefer the senior pastor to preach or the <u>associate pastor</u>?

The stress on the title may lead the respondent to state that person regardless of actual opinion. Similar bias can be the result of indiscreet nods and other forms of gestures which serve to encourage one answer over another. When an answer or opinion is expressed, give a positive and friendly response, urging him or her to go on. Don't express any surprise at their answers.

The attitudes and behavior of the interviewers will usually influence the responses. The person who gets the best and most useful information is the one who is really interested in the work and is keen on getting the most accurate responses. We need to analyze our attitudes toward the people who are being interviewed. A lack of respect will be communicated in many subtle ways, but this will be noticed by the respondents and their cooperation will be influenced. It is your attitudes that guide your behavior, your way of asking questions, your dress, your language and your responses. People will sense this and a negative attitude and lack of respect will alienate the respondent. *Ideal*

Some Fundamentals of Personal Interviewing

1. *Go only to the houses you have been assigned.*
2. *Use a friendly and neutral introduction to gain cooperation.*
3. *Do everything you can to complete the interview once you have found someone home.*
4. *Remember your role is to uncover opinion, not to change it.*
5. *Conduct the interview in a natural, conversational manner.*
6. *Ask the questions only as they are worded.*
7. *Record answers fully as they are given.*
8. *Follow all directions on the questionnaire.*
9. *Ask every question, no matter how sensitive it appears to be.*
10. *Probe where answers are not fully given.*
11. *Record the respondent's own words.*
12. *Writing must be legible.*
13. *Use parentheses to indicate interviewer's words and observations.*
14. *Find a comfortable place where writing is easy.*

Figure 10. 2
Fundamentals of Interviewing

RECORD THE RESPONSES IN AN IN-DEPTH INTERVIEW

If we are conducting a straight interview using a complete questionnaire, it is fairly easy to get an accurate report of the interview. If it is an in-depth interview where the interviewer can probe, then the questions as well as the answers must be recorded. There should be plenty of space on the form for reporting observations by the interviewer. The answers may be recorded by either the interviewer or by an assistant.

(1) *Recording responses by the interviewer.* If the interviewer has to fill in the answers during an in-depth interview, it may make the situation rather difficult and destroy a line of thought. One way is to use two people, one asking the questions and the other writing down the responses, but if it is a sensitive issue, the respondent may be more frank if only one person is present. A questionnaire will be able to help so that answers can be checked, but that could also hinder responses in areas not covered by the questionnaire. In some cases, it may be possible to record the session on tape and transcribe it later. *need to be comfortable — Just for me —*

(2) *Self-administered questionnaires.* If the person is literate, he or she can fill out a questionnaire and anonymity can be safeguarded. If it is a personal interview, the person is known to the interviewer, and true anonymity cannot be promised. A good alternative is to conduct the test with a group of people, and then let each one fill out a form. In this way the anonymity of the person can be kept to encourage frank responses. Let each person fill out a form before any discussion in the group, so that responses will not be influenced by the insights of just a few people. *ask some questions 1st*

EVALUATING THE DATA

The technical term for this is *cleaning the data.* Careful checking of the completed questionnaires needs to be done to assure that guidelines were followed. The work of interviewers may be unsatisfactory due to the following:

- *Falsified results.* This could be cases in which the interviewer has filled out the questionnaires.
- *Inappropriate questioning.* The interviewer may not have asked all the questions on the form.
- *Wrong respondents.* This would be a situation in which the interviewer has substituted a certain respondent with another person.
- *Wrong setting.* The interviewer may have conducted the interview in a group, but the instructions called for individual responses.

If any of these problems are detected, the gathered data needs to be checked for accuracy or destroyed altogether.

Editing will also need to be done to make sure that all data entered into the computer are accurate. Some questionnaires are not complete so they may have to be discarded. Instructions for editing and coding will be covered in the following chapter.

If the questionnaire contains open-ended questions, then each answer needs to be *coded*. Normally you would read through a number of answers to get a sense of the possible answers. Then develop a code for these possible answers and apply the code to answers given on the questionnaires. Obviously such coding is very time consuming so it is strongly recommended that questionnaires are pre-coded.

SAMPLE ILLUSTRATION OF INTERVIEWER GUIDE

A portion of the interviewer guide prepared for the study of adults in Vancouver is given on the following pages as an example. It contains a brief but comprehensive review of the elements of effective interviewing.

Illustration: Interviewer Guide for Vancouver Reachout Survey[3]

Jesus walked and lived among the people of His time. Thus, He was enabled to use words, parables, examples which spoke directly to their needs and backgrounds. In this sense, Jesus was using an excellent form of audience research: observation. This survey project has precisely the same objective: a focusing on the Word of God to speak effectively to modern man. The difference, of course, is that the objective calls for reaching millions and hence different methods of research and communication are required.

The survey has always been used by communicators, although the onset of questionnaire and sampling methods is a modern phe-

---

3. James F. Engel, *How Can I Get Them to Listen?* Grand Rapids: Zondervan, 1977:125–128.

nomenon. It is basically a tool of inquiry and nothing more. Because the goal is to *understand* other people and to grasp their backgrounds and points of view, all involved in this project must strive for objectivity. Objectivity, in turn, requires that certain rules of interviewing practice be followed. This guide is prepared for that purpose.

Some Fundamentals of Effective Interviewing

1. *Go only to the houses you have been assigned.* Each interviewer will be given a list of homes which are eligible to be interviewed. You are not free to substitute other homes without approval from the Reachout office. The reason for this is that we have gone to great expense and effort to guarantee that we will have a representative sample of the Greater Vancouver area. Unless we follow this rule, we could easily wind up with a distorted picture.

2. *Use a friendly and neutral introduction to gain cooperation.* We would suggest you use an introduction something like this:

   "Hello, I'm _____. I'm part of a group of greater Vancouver residents who are working with "People to People." We are from community groups and churches of all types, and we are taking a survey with thousands all over the city to find out basic community needs and concerns. This will only take a few minutes. May I come in?"

   Experiment a bit with this and find out what works for you. Be natural, and be yourself. Display your badge prominently. If there is reluctance, share the introduction letter. Also, we are fully registered with police and other agencies. Occasionally people will check to see.

3. *Do everything you can to complete the interview once you have found someone home.* There often will be some reluctance to go ahead, but a natural, friendly attitude on your part will be a great help. Assure them that all replies are completely anonymous. Call back again at a better time if necessary. Make an appointment right then, and keep it!

4. *Remember your role is to uncover opinion, not to change it.* We want to discover spiritual awareness, interest, and beliefs. Change will occur later as we get into the Reachout program. This is *not* an opportunity for evangelism. If you have an open door for that, call back later on your own.

5. *Conduct the interview in a natural, conversational manner.* Just be yourself.

6. *Ask the questions only as they are worded.* This is very important. Just a slight change of wording can lead to a very different meaning. Therefore, read the question only as it is asked on your questionnaires. If it is not understood, repeat the question just as it is worded. Do not attempt to explain it! If there is no understanding, just leave blank and go on.

7. *Record answers fully as they are given.* Usually all we require is a check mark in the proper place. A few are structured as "open-ended." Do everything you can to get down the exact words. *Listen carefully!* Try to capture what they say, not what you think they said. So record it fully at the time, and do not attempt to change it later. Memory can play tricks. It is helpful to check these answers over to be sure your handwriting is legible, but adding comments should be done only when you are sure you missed something they actually said.

8. *Follow all directions on the questionnaire.* Question order, for example, CANNOT BE CHANGED. Do it exactly as it appears. There are good reasons for everything that is being done.

9. *Ask every question, no matter how sensitive it appears to be.* Every item of information is important.

10. *Probe where answers are not fully given.* This applies only on the open-ended questions. Use a neutral probe such as "Can you tell me more?" "Is there anything else?" Be careful not to comment as they comment. It is absolutely wrong to say something like: "Yes, that's a good idea," etc. Only use neutral probes. Anything other than that can change opinion rather than reflect it.

The Sample

In the community survey, we are attempting to complete 2500 interviews with adults. Your list of homes will have many more than the 13 we wish you to contact. This is because we inevitably will find some who are not at home no matter how many times we try or who just will not cooperate. Therefore, you are free to substitute the next name on the list each time this happens.

Let's assume you have called on a home and no one is home. Try again *one other time* at a different time of day. Much of our work will have to be done in the evening or we will wind up with too many housewives. If a call back produces no response, go to the next name. Do the same if you have a refusal.

We want you to attempt to get about half men and half women in your 13 completed surveys. Do everything you can to bring this about, recognizing that women sometimes are more willing to cooperate than men. Calling as a couple, however, really reduces this reluctance. *Never* interview both husband and wife in a given home. Interview just one person per home.

Conducting the Interview
Try to get in the home. Sometimes this is difficult, but most people invite you in. Then, ask the name of the person you are interviewing. Almost always this should be the man or woman of the house only. Find a comfortable location where you can be uninterrupted if possible. If the television is blaring or kids are making a ruckus, suggest another location. Usually the best bet is to suggest the kitchen or dining room table in that case.

Try to get your respondent (either male or female) alone. If others are there, point out that you are trying to get individual responses. Be tactful about this. If you are calling as husband and wife, one partner quickly can divert the distracters.

Only one person should conduct the interview. The wife may want to carry the ball most of the time, although this is up to you. The other partner sits quietly and does not get involved.

A Guide for Interviewers:
Vancouver Reachout Survey

11

TABULATION AND DATA PROCESSING

Data Collection in the Field
Tabulation and Analysis of Data
Interpretation and Reporting

When the questionnaires have been completed by the field researchers or received through the mail, they need to be tabulated and analyzed in order to provide information regarding our research objectives and in turn help management make the right decisions. The raw data need to be edited, coded, and entered into a computer program before we can begin the actual task of data analysis.

DATA EDITING

The primary purpose of editing is to assure that the data collected is accurate and usable, and that all questions have been answered and forms filled out as instructed. The following is a useful checklist for the editor:

Is the handwriting legible? The responses must be clear so that they are easy to read by the person who will enter the data. If the data is obtained through personal interviews, the interviewer may be able to assist in clarifying unreadable handwriting, but for anonymous questionnaires, the editor will either have to rewrite the answers or the data will need to be handled as missing data.

Are all questions answered? The editor will check the questionnaire for completeness. If only a few questions are left unanswered, it may be possible to just treat it as missing data. If many questions are left unanswered, the editor may decide to discard the form altogether.

Are responses consistent? The editor will carefully check consistencies. Some inconsistencies may be obvious to spot, others may be identified through questions on the form that were designated to provide cross checks of responses. If there are consistent contradictions in responses, the form will probably need to be discarded.

Is the data accurate? The editor will need to be attentive to possible inaccuracies in the data. Comparison of forms completed by different interviewers may give clues as to possible problems, and if direct dishonesty is discovered, the form will need to be discarded.

Is there need for clarification? In open-ended questions it may be difficult to read the entry or the respondent may have used abbreviations not readily understood. On a self-administered questionnaire, it could also be a problem if two answers are checked on a multi-choice question where only one check is acceptable.

CODING

It has been suggested in preceding chapters that questionnaires should be precoded for easy data entry. If this has been done, then the issue of coding is made considerably easier.

Coding is the task of assigning numbers to answers so that they can be easily tabulated and analyzed on a computer. If, for example, a question asked,

Do you live in an urban or a rural area? _____.

Then the respondent will have written in an answer. The editor will then need to assign a code to the answer. For example, if the answer was *urban* it would be coded as a "1," and if the answer was *rural*, it would be a "2."

On the other hand, if the questionnaire had been precoded, the question on the form would have looked something like this:

Do you live in an urban or a rural area? (check one)

    (1) ___ urban

    (2) ___ rural

No further coding will then be necessary, as the person entering the data can read the code on the form.

It is also helpful if all questions on a questionnaire are numbered consecutively. By each question we understand each request for information. The following illustration shows that each question is numbered and each answer is precoded. There may have been twelve questions prior to this one, and then the first question would be number 13. If the questionnaire is divided up into several sections, it is easier to tabulate if a consecutive numbering is observed rather than beginning with number 1 on each section. This will avoid confusion in data analysis and tabulation.

For each of the following sentences, please indicate how true this is of your situation.	Not really (1)	Some (2)	Much (3)	Very much (4)
1. I am concerned about being able to provide good education for my children.				
2. I have often thought about completely changing my life.				
3. Religion is more important to me today than it was five years ago.				

Figure 11. 1

Example of Precoded Questionnaire

In the coding process, special attention will be given to open-ended questions. If they need to be analyzed in categories, then the normal approach is to read 20–30 responses first and get a feeling of how the answers are given. Then develop a set of categories of responses and assign numbers to these categories. We can then go through all the questionnaires and code the open-ended questions according to these codes.

Alternatively, we do not code open-ended questions but use the responses as quality input to the data. It may be helpful to quote certain responses directly in the final report.

There are some helpful suggestions for assigning codes to questions:

- *Make codes mutually exclusive so* that answers can only fit into one code category. No piece of data should be able to fit into more than one code.
- *Make codes collectively exhaustive* so that all answers can fit into one of the code categories. A code for "other" can be used to safeguard this point.
- *Keep details* so that analysis of various sub-points can be done at a later stage if necessary. It is always possible to combine code categories later when details are not required for a certain tabulation.
- *Number the completed forms and keep the same number on the computer entry or card*. This will make it possible to check the data entry later if problems of inaccuracy or inconsistency is discovered during data analysis.

DATA ENTRY

The most simple form of data entry is, of course, to count all responses and write them on a blank questionnaire. Even though it is often helpful to have the data written in on a blank form, the activity involved is rather cumbersome, especially if there are many forms to be counted. It is therefore important to have a system for data entry where analysis is fairly simple. This does then require a computer-readable form of some kind.

The traditional computer entry format was to enter the data on a computer card. On such a card, each response was assigned a row on a card with eighty vertical columns. The data codes were punched into the card. The computer could then count the responses to each answer and the necessary tabulations could take place. Even though this method is pretty much outdated for computer analysis, the system is important, and it can be adapted for hand tabulation where only a small number of questionnaires are involved.

Today we have quite sophisticated software that can help reduce the work significantly. Responses can even be read into the computer through an optical reader, but normally the data is entered manually. For some simple analysis, we could even use a spreadsheet program, but it is easier to use programs specifically designated for the purpose of analyzing questionnaires.

STRUCTURE OF COMPUTER FILE

In this section we will refer to a statistical program called ABstat.[1] Apart from general statistical packages, the program is also prepared for analysis of questionnaires.

The first step is to create a structure for entry of data into a computer file. If questionnaires are precoded, much of the conceptualization will have taken place earlier, and the creation of a structure is fairly easy. In the ABstat program you simply go into the program and select *Create New File*. Then you select *Structure Edit* and the program will give you a format to follow. For each variable, you write a name of up to ten letters. It is strongly advised that the variable numbers follow exactly the numbers on the questionnaire to make entry easier and corrections and checking much more simple. If the name of the variable can be as close to the question as possible, it will be easier to understand the basic print out of the entries. For example, to the question, Where do you live?, the variable name could just be *Location* or something like that.

The computer will also ask for the following information: (1) *Type* and the choices are *character* (text) or *numerical*; (2) *Length* to indicate how many spaces would be necessary for the response. This could be 1 where codes do not go beyond 9, or it could be 4, if a year needs to be written in. For open-ended questions that are not coded, you may want twenty or more spaces; (3) *Decimal* to indicate if decimals are needed in the entry; (4) *Choice Tables* are for use in cross tabulations. These can be defined later; (5) *Long Description* is for entry of the whole question or some other kind of desired description.

If decimals are not needed for an entry, and if you decide to define choice tables later, then all you need to do is write the variable name, identify character or numerical, and state number of spaces needed. The rest can

---

1. AndersonBell, *Abstat*, Statistical package for Windows, Release 1.90. Anderson-Bell Corp., PO Box 5160, Arvada, CO 80006, USA. 1994.

be just "enter," and the program jumps to the next variable. For well-prepared questionnaires, the creation of a structure will be done very quickly.

As an illustration of the program, a small program consisting of only five variables has been created (figure 11.2).

Structure List							
Var	Name	Type	Pos	Length	Dec	Choice Tbl	Descrip
1	Age	N	1	2	0		
2	Education	C	3	8			
3	Income	N	11	1	0		
4	Gender	N	12	1	0		
5	Family	N	13	1	0		
6							

Figure 11. 2
Structure List

ENTERING DATA

After saving the structure, the next phase will be actual *data entry*. On the program select *Data Edit*. The program will automatically give you a clean form for data entry. All you need to do is enter the codes for each variable.

It is strongly recommended that each case, that is, each record will follow the same numbers as you have entered on the questionnaires. The computer will automatically start with number one and then go on to number two. The entry process is made easy as the program automatically jumps to next entry.

Straight Tabulation of Data

A direct printout of a *Data List* will be useful. On a data list, all cases are printed and the data is provided as is. This is helpful for spotting possible problems with codes or entry mistakes. For our illustration, we have entered data from ten records.

```
Data Edit
Rec: 3
     Var      Name
      1        Age
      2      Education
      3       Income
      4       Gender
      5       Family
```

Figure 11. 3
Data Entry Form on ABstat Program

Command: LIST					
Rec	Age	Education	Income	Gender	Family
1	28	Primary	3	1	3
2	31	Primary	2	1	2
3	23	Secondary	4	2	1
4	38	None	2	1	4
5	34	None	3	2	2
6	30	Primary	3	2	2
7	29	None	2	2	1
8	30	Primary	4	1	2
9	28	Primary	2	1	3
10	27	Secondary	4	1	2

Figure 11. 4
Data List

Frequency Count

The most helpful tabulation is usually a frequency count of the answers given by the entire sample. In order to analyze subsets, for example differences between rural and urban, you can ask the computer to give you a print out of such subsets for comparison. The computer can print out both the numbers and percentages as well as preparing a simple graph of the results as seen in figure 11.5 where we have selected the variables *education* and *family* from the data in figures 11.3 and 11.4.

It is helpful to transfer both the frequency counts and the percentages directly onto a copy of the questionnaire itself so that responses can be grasped at a glance.

If we are dealing with data from a semantic differential scale, it is usually best to combine the two extreme response categories on each end of the scale into one. As was mentioned earlier, many people will not utilize the extreme scale positions, and the frequencies of extreme positions will be unduly small.

```
Frequency Report of Education
                       0                  25                50
   Value  Freq     %  |-+-|-+-|-+-|-+-|-+-|-+-|-+-|-+-|-+-|
    None   3     30.0 |***************
 Primary   5     50.0 |*************************
Secondary  2     20.0 |**********
   Total  10    100.0 |-+-|-+-|-+-|-+-|-+-|-+-|-+-|-+-|-+-|
                       0                  25                50

Frequency Report of Family
                       0                  25                50
   Value  Freq     %  |-+-|-+-|-+-|-+-|-+-|-+-|-+-|-+-|-+-|
      1    2     20.0 |**********
      2    4     40.0 |********************
      3    3     30.0 |***************
      4    1     10.0 |*****
   Total  10    100.0 |-+-|-+-|-+-|-+-|-+-|-+-|-+-|-+-|-+-|
                       0                  25                50
```

Figure 11. 5
Frequency Count

CROSS-TABULATION

Straight tabulations are helpful in providing a general picture, but the underlying dynamics are obscured. We cannot segregate the responses in one subgroup from those in another. This is the purpose of cross-tabulation. For example, we may want to know if there is a difference between how satisfied women are with the worship service with that of male members. Or, we may want to study different Bible reading patterns among church members.

The usual starting point is to cross-classify answers by demographic characteristics, especially age, sex, and socioeconomic status. Variations may provide clues to differences in receptivity between audience subgroups and the best ways to reach them.

It is usually helpful to cross-tabulate the main subgroups with the key measures of our study. Often these are questions centering on meaning and purpose. The goal could, for example, be to differentiate those who are seeking new meaning in life from those who are not. The result is a clear picture of all responses given by seekers and those given by the non-seekers.

		Very much	Much	Some	Nei-ther	Some	Much	Very Much	
52.	Worth looking up to	26	25	108	171	14	6	12	Not worth looking up to
53.	Fool	12	12	43	172	55	33	25	Clever
54.	Important	33	44	91	155	14	5	12	Not important
55.	Useful	30	79	114	107	15	5	10	Useless
56.	Sell nation	11	6	21	107	66	62	53	Love nation
57.	Enduring	63	97	51	103	8	10	14	Not enduring
58.	Love neighbors	45	80	75	115	12	5	6	Hate neighbors
59.	Sad	12	12	38	111	67	62	33	Happy

Figure 11. 6
Entry of all Data on Semantic Differential Scale

STATISTICAL ANALYSIS

There are numerous statistical formulas available for treatment of our data. In the ABstat program, many of these can be selected by simply clicking the type needed. This presupposes that the researcher will know the kind of data being analyzed and the kind of statistics that can be applied to that kind of data.[2] Usually an experienced researcher or statistician is needed to assist with this.

For example, we have three different measures for *central tendency*: mean, median, and mode. They need to be used according to the type of data available.

A useful statistical procedure to test whether differences between two or more percentages are due to chance variations is called the *Chi-square test*. This statistical method will be used in the following example.

EXAMPLE OF CHI-SQUARE ANALYSIS

The following case provides an example of a cross-classification table in which readership of four Christian magazines is analyzed by age.[3] For purposes of simplicity, only two age categories are used.

Notice, first of all, that the cross-classification variable is placed across the top of the table. The percentages are computed downward by columns, i.e., the column total is utilized as the percentage base. This is the usual procedure in cross-classification analysis. The row totals are nothing more than the straight tabulation of readership for each magazine.

Magazines	Age Category					
	Under 35		*35 and Over*		*Total*	
	No.	%	No.	%	No.	%
A	60	30.0%	280	35.0%	340	34.0%
B	40	20.0%	170	21.3%	210	21.0%
C	30	15.0%	40	5.0%	70	7.0%

2. See chapter 9 for a chart with different kinds of data and applicable statistics.
3. This example is provided in James F. Engel, *How Can I Get Them to Listen?* Zondervan, 1977:134–140. The example is inserted here with permission from the author.

| D | 70 | 35.0% | 310 | 38.7% | 380 | 38.0% |
| Total | 200 | 100.0% | 800 | 100.0% | 1000 | 100.0% |

Figure 11. 7
Christian Magazine Readership Cross-Classified by Age

Now, what does this table tell us? First, there are some readership differences between age groups. Younger respondents (those under 35), in particular, seem to prefer magazine C. Yet the differences are not large. There is an obvious need for further analysis, and the next step is to evaluate these differences statistically.

Statistical Analysis

Our first step is an **Analysis of Confidence Intervals**. Let's return, for a moment, to the straight tabulation using the above example. Here the data tell us that 34 percent read magazine A, 21 percent read magazine B, 7 percent read magazine C, and 38 percent read magazine D. How representative is this of the total target population (or universe, to use the statistician's term)?

The reader will recall the discussion of confidence intervals in an earlier chapter. There always is a range of error which must be taken into consideration when generalizing from sample data to the population, and this can be measured if random sampling has been used. Assuming our sample was chosen at random, we now can refer to the tables for confidence levels. Here we discover that we can be 95 percent confident that the true figure "out there" is somewhere in the interval of our sample statistic ±3 percent. Therefore, the actual readership of magazine A is somewhere between 31 and 37 percent.

Data interpretation always must take confidence intervals into account. This is especially true if this interval is quite wide, in which case greater caution must be taken in attributing precision to the answers. The books referenced at the end of the chapter are helpful in explaining the computation and interpretation of confidence intervals. Most readers, of course, need not be concerned with these mechanical considerations.

Significance of Differences Between Subgroups. We observed that the differences in readership between the four magazines are not large. In fact, it is possible that these reflect only *chance variations*. If so, then the differences themselves are of no managerial significance. Chance always is a possibility when one is working with data drawn from samples.

Fortunately, it is possible to measure statistically whether or not such differences are due simply to chance. There is a whole family of statistical methods which can be utilized, and each is applicable under precisely stated conditions. Most readers will not be interested in these technical details, and those who are will find help in the sources listed at the end of the book.

There is one statistical method which is widely used to assess the meaning of differences of this type and which is not beyond the grasp of the reader. In words, it is referred to as *chi square analysis*, and usually it is depicted in statistical symbols as follows: X^2. The formula for this statistic is given below, and the reader is urged to put down that inevitable defense mechanism rearing its ugly head from the days of high school algebra. Remember that mathematical notation is merely shorthand for what can be said in words. So, here goes:

$$X^2 = \sum \frac{(O - E)^2}{E} \qquad = 24.799$$

where,

$\sum$ = sum of

O = the actual answer given by members of the subgroup (say, an age group)

E = the answer one would expect members of the subgroup to give if there were no differences from one subgroup to another.

Put in words, it will be necessary to compare the actual observed value (O) in each cell of a table against that value which would be expected (E) if there were no differences from one subgroup to the next. The sixty people in figure 20 under the age of thirty-five who read magazine A thus would be noted as the observed value for that cell of the table and so on. The expected value must be computed, however.

Now, how does one compute the expected value? Looking again at the figures, one would expect that 34 percent of those in each age group would read magazine A if there were no differences between the two groups. The 34-percent figure appears as the total at the end of the first row. And 21 percent would read magazine B and so on. The expected readership of magazine A by those under thirty-five, then, would be sixty-eight, which is 34 percent of 200 (200 is the total number of males in the sample who are under thirty-five). An identical computation is made for each cell in the table, and the results of this simple computation appear in the following figure. Observed values are designated by O and expected values by E.

Magazines	Age Category				
	Under 35		35 and Over		Total
	O	E	O	E	
Total					
A	60	68	280	272	340
B	40	42	170	168	210
C	30	14	40	56	70
D	70	76	310	304	380

Figure 11. 8
A Comparison of Observed and Expected Readership
of Four Christian Magazines Cross-Classified by Age

Now we have the basis to compute X^2. First take the difference between the observed and the expected value for the first cell in the table (readership of magazine A by those under 35). This gives a value of 8. Now, according to the formula, that value should be squared (the number 8 multiplied by itself) and divided by the expected value 68. This is 64 divided by 68 which, in turn, equals .94. That figure is jotted down, and an identical computation is made for all remaining cells in the table. Then all of these figures are summed into one total, and that gives us the computed value of X^2. In this example, $X^2 = 24.799$.

We now have to make one more simple computation and we then are ready to determine if these differences in readership are real or merely are the result of chance variations. We count the number of rows in the table and subtract 1 from that figure (4 - 1 = 3). We do the same for the number of columns, not counting the total as a column (2 - 1 = 1). Now we multiply these two figures and this gives what the statistician has labeled the number of *degrees of freedom*. The formula for degrees of freedom is (r-1)(c-1), where "r" is the number of rows and "c" the number of columns. The number of degrees of freedom in our sample, then, is 3 (3x1).

Degrees of Freedom	Critical Value
1	3.841
2	5.991
3	7.815
4	9.488
5	11.07
6	12.59
7	14.07
8	15.51
9	16.92
10	18.31
11	19.68
12	21.03
13	22.36
14	23.68
15	25.00
16	26.30
17	27.59
18	28.87
19	30.14
20	31.41

The bigger the difference the more significant.

Can help support the data

Figure 11. 9
A Portion of X^2 Table Showing the Critical Values at the 95% Confidence Level for Degrees of Freedom Ranging from 1–20.

Now we are ready to consult the X^2 table, a portion of which is reproduced in figure 11.9. It gives what is known as the *critical value* for each degree of freedom. If our computed chi square value exceeds that figure, there is less than a 5 percent chance that differences as large as those observed in the data are due to chance. We then can safely assume in the example used here that there is a real difference in magazine preference and readership from one age group to the next. Notice that the critical value for 3 degrees of freedom is 7.815, whereas our computed value is 24.799. It is apparent that these differences may not be explained away by chance. To use the statistician's terms, we may conclude that the differences are *statistically significant* (not due to chance).

It is possible that one would have thousands of cross-tabulation tables in a large-scale computer analysis. The first step is to go through and assess which, if any, are statistically significant as we have done here. If this is not possible, focus only on those tables in which the differences obviously are so large that they could not be due to chance.

LOGICAL INTERPRETATION

Now that chance has been rejected as the explanation, let's refer back to the original data (figure 11.7) to detect the source of the variations. The differences in readership between magazines A, B, and D by members of these two age groups are not great. The largest difference is 10 percent with magazine C. It is favored by readers under age 35 more than it is by their older counterparts.

This is a good illustration of the fact that statistical significance (i.e., rejection of chance) does not necessarily imply *managerial significance*. In other words, one could legitimately conclude that readership differences of this magnitude do not warrant changes in strategy. Usually the author follows the general rule that responses in any given subgroup must deviate from those given by the total sample by at least 10 percent before serious consideration is given to changes in strategy. Obviously there will be instances in which such a rule should be modified, but it is an acceptable general guideline.

SOME CONSIDERATIONS REGARDING DATA INTERPRETATION

The following suggestions by Engel are helpful reminders of how to deal with data.[4]

1. *Do not attempt to produce "startling results." Often the outcome will be nothing more than confirmation of the expected. There is no reason to expect that research always will uncover something that is dramatically new.*

2. *Do not overemphasize favorable evidence. Always check to see that all evidence is reported. Sometimes there will be hesitance to stress the negative, especially if it will place a client in a bad light.*

3. *Do not be dazzled by complexity. There are some researchers who use statistical terms as a "snow job." The uninitiated reader may conclude that data are valid for this reason alone, when quite the opposite may, in fact, be the case. Simplicity and clarity are the hallmarks of the sensitive, managerially-oriented researcher.*

4. *Do not place too much faith in averages. These are only a measure of central tendency, and the great range of underlying response can be obscured.*

5. *Do not mistake respondent opinion for fact. What the person thinks is never an infallible indication of the true situation. This, of course, is not to say that attitudes and opinions are of no value in research. It merely places this kind of information in perspective.*

---

4. Ibid., p. 140.

12

INTERPRETATION AND REPORTING

Tabulation and Analysis of Data
Interpretation and Reporting
Implementation of Findings

Throughout the research project, research objectives and associated information needs have guided us through sampling procedures, questionnaire design, field work, and cross tabulations. Now the gathered data need to be interpreted in relation to information needs and the original decision problem. Data as such may be interesting, but it is more or less useless unless it is interpreted and becomes information on which you can base your decisions.

Interpretation will be a joint exercise of the researcher and management. Both will need to be included in the interpretation process to safeguard appropriate understanding and application. The researcher will want to underline the basis for interpretations during the presentation of the findings.

The presentation of research findings will consist of two parts, a written report and an oral presentation. For each presentation, we need to remember that we are in a communication situation, and as such our first consideration is the audience. Who will be my reader? Who will be my listener? Writing research reports and providing effective oral presentations are skills that a researcher learns by experience. But there are a number of guidelines that can help a novice to prepare a good report and presentation.

PRESENTING THE RESULTS OF RESEARCH

A final challenge to the researcher is therefore to be able to communicate the results of a research project in such a way that it will be seen as important to the management or leaders of the organization that has requested the research. They are the ones who will phase the results into a strategy.

All the rules and guidelines for effective written and oral communication are important at this stage, or all the work and energy given to the research project will be wasted. If the researcher approaches this challenge from a communicator's perspective he or she will aim at developing a trust relationship with the readers and listeners.

A written report is a presentation of the findings, but it will also include all necessary background information that will help validate the results. It is prepared specifically for those who are going to make decisions, but a secondary audience will always be other researchers who may at a later time want to build on the foundations laid in this study.

For many leaders, the research report will be their main source of information regarding the study. The report is also a way of showing the usefulness of having good and reliable information on which decisions can be reached.

Decision-makers may not be too interested in all the background information and details of the research. They will focus on the primary information provided and how that relates to solving present problems. They will try to see how the information can help them reach critical decisions that are necessary for the organization to succeed. On the other hand, it is important that enough details are provided so that they can judge the validity of the study.

PREPARING THE WRITTEN REPORT

As the purpose of a research study will differ from project to project, there will, consequently, not be two research reports that are exactly alike. But there is a series of guidelines that can be given as to how a report should be prepared. These do again follow general guidelines on communication.

Who Is the Reader?

The primary audience for the research report is the decision-maker so the presentation of information should obviously be tailor-made for that purpose. If the research has been done on the basis of the suggestions in this book, there will be clear and accurate objectives for the research, objectives based on the needs of the organization. If these have been followed, then the decision-makers are interested in seeing how the research can provide exact and helpful information on how to solve specific problems or how to plan the ministry. The report needs to be interesting and exciting to read, and research jargon should be avoided whenever possible. As you work on preparing the research report, the objectives of the research and the needs and interests of the reader should be kept in mind at all times.

Be Short, Clear, and Complete

The reporting of research findings requires a certain type of presentation. The report itself must be complete so that all the necessary information is included, but it has to be presented in such a way that unnecessary details will not cloud the main points. Include all important information in the main body of the report and leave information of secondary importance in an appendix.

Objective Presentation

It is obvious that a researcher will want to be effective in his or her presentation of the findings, but the presentation must be completely objective. All information needs to be presented in a way that is not distorted or slanted in any way so any attempt at selling or manipulating the results will be interpreted as deception. This requirement of objectivity does not mean that the report cannot be written in a creative and interesting way, and obviously main points and findings will have a priority treatment in a research report.

Every researcher will from time to time be in a situation where the information gathered will not be favorable to the policies of the organization or to the interest of the leaders. Findings may cut across previous experience or general interests of a decision-maker. It is the requirement and the responsibility of the researcher to keep the objectivity and then try to present the findings in a convincing manner that will prove to those receiving the report that the presentation is valid. It will always be up to the management to decide if research findings should be applied and phased into strategy decisions.

OUTLINE FOR WRITTEN REPORT

Most written reports will be able to use the following outline:

1. *Title Page*
2. *Table of Contents*
3. *Table of Figures*
4. *Executive Summary*
5. *Main Body of the Report*
   * *Introduction to the Report*
   * *Methodology That Has Been Followed*
   * *Obtained Results*
   * *Description of Research Limitations*
6 *Interpretation and Recommendations*
7. *Appendix*

Title Page

The cover or title page should clearly state the title of the study and in its name or description outline the main purpose or content of the study. The report must be dated and the name of the organization that has sponsored the research also needs to be on the title page. Name of researcher or research organization will also be provided. If the research is confidential that confidentiality will be guarded by putting the names of those who receive copies on the cover of the report.

Table of Contents

The purpose of having a table of contents is to assist the reader in finding information on particular points. The function is therefore one of reference and it should be able to be used as such. If several different topics are covered, then reference to these topics and page numbers should be provided.

Table of Figures

A research report will often have several tables and figures that illustrate the situation and findings. It is helpful to have a list of such tables and figures for easy reference by page number.

Executive Summary

All research reports should have a brief, one- to three-page executive summary at the beginning. The executive summary will obviously be written after the main body of the report has been prepared. It is the most important part of the research report as this will probably be the only part of the report that will be read by all decision-makers or board members.

The executive summary will be an overview of the research report and it should clearly state the purpose of the report and what the key findings were. Again, the findings will have to be put in the perspective of the objectives and information needs. The executive summary needs to be action-oriented so that decision-makers can be aided in phasing the report into strategy. This means that key results are presented along with conclusions and recommendations. The executive summary will not include any tables or figures, but should be written in an easy and action-oriented style.

Main Body of the Report

This section is by far the largest part of the report and it will contain several points.

a. **Introduction to the Report**. The researcher should remember that many decision-makers may have forgotten the details of the problem that called for research in the first case, why it was necessary, and what the objectives and the information needs were. The introduction will therefore explain the nature of the problem and the objectives of the research project.

b. **Methodology That Has Been Followed**. The methodology section is primarily included to validate the research findings. It will carefully describe the research design, how and why it was developed this way, the sampling plan selected and used, and a description of the data collection form and its use in the field. It will also include the statistical formulas and approaches used to tabulate the data. In this section, a researcher may be tempted to use technical jargon that accurately describes the methodology used, but as the reader will most likely not be familiar with such terms, every attempt must be made to make the text communicative. Secondary material, sampling plans, and other helpful material can be put into the appendix.

The methodology section should also be written in such a way that another researcher would be able to duplicate the research if necessary or to test the conclusions.

c. **Obtained Results**. This section will be the main section of the research report and the one that will command greatest interest. It is necessary to organize the data around research objectives so that there will be an easy correspondence. In the body of the report all important data will be presented. Remaining information not used in the body of the report can be put in the appendix. The report itself must be seen as a whole with logical steps and illustrations. Often the presentation will include cross tabulations for easy comparisons.

In the presentation of data, a researcher can use a number of different approaches. There will, of course, be text, but this can be illustrated and helped by tables and figures, and in particular by graphs that demonstrate the findings. A researcher will need to evaluate how much should be included and which kind of presentation is needed.

When tables are used, careful headings and descriptions need to be attached so that a reader will not have to read the main text of the report in order to understand a given table. Each table must communicate by itself. The discussion of the table in the text can then focus on patterns and trends.

	1st Qtr	2nd Qtr	3rd Qtr	4th Qtr
Men	120	110	90	125
Women	130	120	115	135
Children	55	50	30	60

Figure 12. 1
Illustration of Table

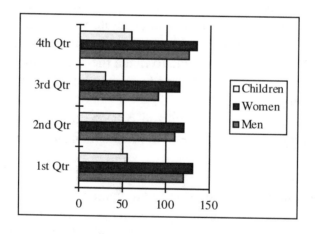

Figure 12. 2
Illustration of Bar Chart

Often the use of a bar chart is helpful. It is much easier to compare sizes of responses on a graphical presentation. A bar chart is easy to make and easy to interpret. This is illustrated on figures 12.1 and 12.2. The data from the table in figure 12.1 is presented on a bar chart in figure 12.2.

A pie chart is often used to indicate size of responses as a portion of a total figure. This can be percentages.

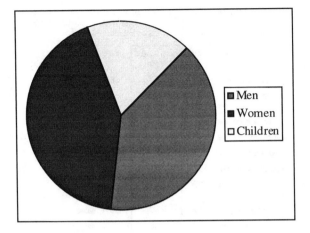

Figure 12. 3
Illustration of Pie Chart

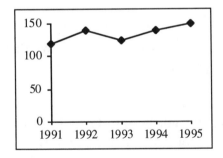

Figure 12. 4
Illustration of Line Chart

It is often interesting to have a line chart instead of a bar chart. This can, for example, be an illustration of church membership growth or decline over a long period of time. This will show trends in membership and show if there has been a rapid increase or maybe even a slow attrition.

For the purpose of easy analysis and presentation of data, it is also helpful to restructure the semantic differential scale so that all positive variables are on one side and negative variables on the other side. Figure 12.5 illustrates this point,

"Please give your opinion concerning those who
follow the Christian religion. Indicate on each
line the answer that you feel is most correct."

	[very, much, some] much	neither	[some, much, very] much	
Worth look-ing up to	▬▬▬▬ 40%	43%	░8% ▬	Not worth look-ing up to
Clever	▬▬▬ 28%	43%	17% ▬▬	Fool
Important	▬▬▬ 42%	39%	8% ▬	Not important
Useful	▬▬▬▬▬ 56%	27%	7% ▬	Useless
Love nation	▬▬▬▬ 45%	27%	1o% ▬▬	"Sell nation"
Enduring	▬▬▬▬ 53%	26%	8% ▬	Not enduring
Love neigh-bors	▬▬▬▬ 5o%	29%	6% ▬	Hate neighbors
Happy	▬▬▬ 41%	28%	16% ▬▬	Sad
Joyful	▬▬▬▬ 48%	3o%	7% ▬	Gloomy
(Rich	▬▬ 20%	5o%	14% ▬▬	Poor)
Good friend	▬▬▬▬ 51%	3o%	6% ▬	Poor friend
Have many friends	▬▬▬▬ 45%	34%	7% ▬	Lonesome
Good	▬▬▬▬ 48%	34%	5% ▬	Bad

Figure 12. 5

Illustration of Semantic Differential Scale with Positive Variables
on One Side. Also, All Positive Answers Have Been Collapsed and
the Same for Negative Answers.

d. **Description of Research Limitations**. In every research project
there are things that do not work out the way it was intended. There might
have been problems with the design, or there might have been limitations
related to sampling. The researcher may also have discovered biased
questions in the research instrument. It is important to be frank about such
limitations and describe them in the report. During the oral presentation, a
researcher will indicate the weaknesses and also clearly state where conclusions and recommendations are affected by the limitations.

Interpretations, Conclusions, and Recommendations

In the process of presenting data and results, there will most likely have
been a number of interpretations and conclusions, but it is important to
summarize these in relation to the objectives and information needs.

Based on the interpretation given, it would be important for the researcher to highlight possible implications of the findings and how such implications could be phased into strategy. A researcher should, if possible, provide recommendations to the decision-makers and show possible implications of using the data.

Appendix

All information that is not essential to the body of the report should be put in the appendix. This could include a copy of the questionnaire itself and a listing of all data. It is usually helpful to have a questionnaire with all obtained data written on it for easier reference and there could also be copies of the questionnaire with data from subsets of the sample.

Sampling plans can also be provided in the appendix, and if use has been made of secondary data or references have been made to other research studies, it may be important to include such information in the appendix. If there have been special instructions developed for field interviewers, a set of such instructions can also be provided in the appendix. And all data, tables, and statistical information not presented in the body should be put in the appendix as well.

ORAL PRESENTATION

The presentation of the research report in person through an oral presentation is of utmost importance. Often the oral presentation will be the deciding factor as to whether a research report will be followed or not. The researcher should therefore do what he or she can to arrange for a meeting with the decision-makers, the board, or the group that has requested the research and will be responsible for putting it into action.

The written research report will be available with all the findings. The oral presentation, on the other hand, will focus on key findings. It will help people accept the research, validate the findings, and give help regarding interpretation and application.

A number of tips can be given regarding the preparation of an oral presentation:

1. Be well prepared. A new researcher may want to practice the presentation a few times to gain confidence.
2. Enough copies of the written report should be available to those present, and the researcher will have prepared nice overhead transparencies or posters with the key findings so that they are easy to understand. If tables are presented on overhead transparencies, the size of letters and figures should be such that they can be easily read by all in the room.
3. The personal appearance, dress, and style will also be important in accepting the research.
4. By using overhead transparencies, the researcher can at all times face the audience and keep their attention.
5. A slide presentation or a video may also be helpful for certain projects. If, for example, the research has been conducted in a special area, or there are certain geographical or social factors related to the decision problem, it may be helpful to show such factors on slides or video to the group to focus attention on the key issues.
6. As in other oral presentations, it is important to talk with the audience rather than reading from a paper or from the screen. Talk about the findings and point to key issues rather than read from a text that may be difficult to understand.
7. It is, of course, important that equipment is prepared ahead of time and that it is functioning.
8. A researcher should be well prepared to answer questions. Preliminary discussion with key members of the group can help the researcher to be prepared for questions that may come up.

IMPLEMENTATION OF FINDINGS

This is the last step in the research process. The implementation is totally out of the hands of the researcher. The leadership will decide how the information gained through research will be phased into strategy and application. But, only if implementation of the findings take place can we consider a research project successful.

Section III

SPECIAL APPLICATIONS OF RESEARCH

13

MEDIA RESEARCH

We will in this chapter look at certain areas of media research that are of special interest to our present purpose: (1) research which deals with the medium itself and the selection of media, (2) methods for testing effects of media programs, (3) testing media products and programs through copy testing or pretesting, and (4) program evaluation procedures. Each of these areas have their specific approaches which can readily be used by Christian media researchers.

RESEARCH RELATED TO THE MEDIUM ITSELF

Many management decisions relate to the selection of media or channels of communication. We need to ask questions such as, Which media should we choose: television, radio or newspapers? What specific television time should be selected? Which magazine will reach our intended audience? All such decisions require the availability of data related to the medium itself. The information needed can be categorized as follows:

- Distribution of the Media   *gov. stats*
- Exposure to the Media   *Nielsen etc.*
- Program Exposure   *ratings*
- Message Attention
- Communication Understanding
- Response to Message

FEBC
Research based
on letters –
multiplied
Many illiterate
Can't write letters

A variety of methods are available for media research and many of them can be used by Christian communicators. The last five points above are increasingly more difficult to measure, but, at the same time, they are of increasing importance for the Christian communicator. We need to know if the message is getting through to the intended audience. If the message or ad does not result in overt response, we need to know the reasons. Let us look at the above points in more detail.

Distribution of the Media

This will include such items as the circulation number for a magazine or newspaper or the number of television or radio sets available to carry the message. If you are a producer of audio cassettes, you will also want to know the distribution of cassette players. Distribution data are the most readily attainable and are relatively free of controversy in terms of their accuracy. In most countries, the information can be acquired through secondary sources.

Exposure to the Media

This is the number of people exposed to the medium itself. Here we measure the number of readers who obtain a copy of a given issue of a magazine or newspaper, or the number of television viewers. It is a study of the potential audience size.

Audiences are measured by a wide variety of methods. In the United States television audience statistics are available through rating businesses such as A. C. Nielsen and Arbitron. They are using methods like *diary entries*, *audio meters*, and *telephone panels*. Radio is measured through similar methods. Such measurements are able to give fairly exact data on who watches, when they watch, and which programs they watch. Demographic profiles are prepared for advertisers.

Program Exposure

Here we are dealing with the actual number of people who are exposed to a specific program in the media. People may be exposed to a program or article, but not notice a specific advertisement. The number will probably be much less than the potential audience.

It is possible for an organization or church to conduct such a study through a survey research project. A community could, for example, be surveyed regarding their exposure to certain programs from a local church.

In Pakistan research indicated that an average of ten people had listened to each copy of a Scripture cassette for children. When 2,000 copies had been distributed, then 20,000 people had actually listened to it.[1]

Message Attention

This is the number of people who actually paid attention to the program in question. This could be a *recognition test* where we try to count the number of readers who remember seeing an ad, as well as those who actually read some or all of it. Such an approach has been followed in a study of denominational and evangelistic magazines.[2] It would also be possible to analyze how many people actually paid attention and listened to a sermon.

As attention to a given message is influenced by factors such as color and size of an ad, positioning in the medium, and the topic itself, it is most helpful to study these topics. What was it that caused a person to be attentive to a given message?

Communication Understanding

Not all of those who paid attention to the message will have comprehended the message and committed it to memory. This number is typically less than those perceiving the ad or program. To measure this, we can employ a *recall test* in which the actual amount of content remembered is measured. In a church, we could use such measures to test a sermon or a teaching series.

---

1. Viggo B. Søgaard, *Audio Scriptures Handbook*, United Bible Societies, 1991:Appendix 2.
2. "How to do Readership Surveys." *Christianity Today*, Inc. Research Dept. 1992.

Response to Message

We want to have a clear picture of who and how many people "take buying action" as a result of our program or specific advertisement. We need to know what actually happened, and who took behavioral steps in their spiritual journey towards Christ. In Christian communication we do want to have data on immediate responses, and letters may be an indication of listener response. But we need to go beyond such immediate responses and measure actual long-term effects.

Figure 13. 1
Sample of Magazine Ads
(Reduced in Size)

RESEARCH EXAMPLE: RESPONSE TO CHRISTIAN ADS IN SECULAR MAGAZINES

A good place for an organization to start with research is to discover the reach of present ministry and its effectiveness. The ideal is, of course, to start a ministry on the basis of environmental studies and a clearly defined audience, but if this has not been done, we need to study the present outreach to determine the composition of our audience. Who is my reader/listener/viewer? One such study was an analysis of responses to ads placed in secular magazines by a Christian organization. The study was based on data already available in the files of the organization.[3]

Background Information. A Christian publisher in Bangkok had for a period of time placed Christian ads in secular magazines. The magazines were primarily women's magazines. The ads were general in nature, and carried the common title *Good News for You*. A sample ad (reduced in size) is given in figure 13.1.

The ad included an offer for free literature, and to facilitate response, a coupon was included asking for name, address, and age of the respondent. A code number indicated magazine and type of ad. Over a period of time, approximately 3000 responses had come in from readers. The manager of the organization then asked for research assistance to analyze these responses.

Please send the book "Good News for You" to me FREE
Name _____ Age _____ years
House number _____ Street _____
Town _____ Province _____
Send to: "Good News for You," Post Box 503, Bangkok
001-01

Figure 13. 2
Translation of Coupon Information

response may be a multiple response mechanism —

Purpose and Objectives. The objectives of the analysis were established as follows:

- to describe the people who responded to the ads, so that the organization would be able to serve them better
- to estimate cost-effectiveness of different ads and magazines to aid the organization in the selection of magazines
- to obtain demographic data on people who respond to such use of print media for the purpose of strategy design.

---

3. Viggo B. Søgaard, "Magazine Advertising." Unpublished research report on Christian ads in secular papers.

Tabulation of Data. The following variables were used in the tabulation of results:

- sex of the respondent
- age
- geographical location
- magazine in which the ad was placed
- the ad used

All of this information could all be obtained from the coupons. The organization was also able to provide information concerning the cost of placing each ad in the various magazines. Such cost figures are based on published magazine circulation figures.

Cost Analysis. The data indicated that the best cost-effectiveness was obtained in *Bangkok Weekly*, where the "True Love" ad response averaged 5.05 Baht (approximately U.S. 25 cents). The most expensive was a Cliff Richard ad in *Dan-Thai* magazine where each response averaged 81.81 Baht (approximately U.S. $4.00). As circulation figures supplied by the magazines may be inflated, these figures should be treated with caution. Consequently, the figures are based on actual responses rather than on stated audience exposure.

Magazine and Ad	Number of Responses	Advertising Cost	Cost per Response
001-01	672	3,400	5.05 Baht
001-06	78	2,125	27.24 Baht
002-01	300	3,400	11.33 Baht
002-03	93	2,100	22.58 Baht
002-04	31	1,500	48.38 Baht
003-01	401	3,400	8.47 Baht
004-01	630	3,400	5.39 Baht
004-06	117	2,125	18.16 Baht
005-01	546	3,400	6.22 Baht
005-02	44	3,600	81.81 Baht
006-01	274	3,400	12.40 Baht

Figure 13. 3
Cost Per Response

Age of The Respondents. Prior to the research, the average age of respondents was estimated by the organization to be mid-twenties. Actually, the data showed an average age of 18 for men and 17 for women. We can see in figure 13.4 that the age distribution is narrow, from approximately 12 years of age to a sharp drop at 20, and only a very few above the age of 30.

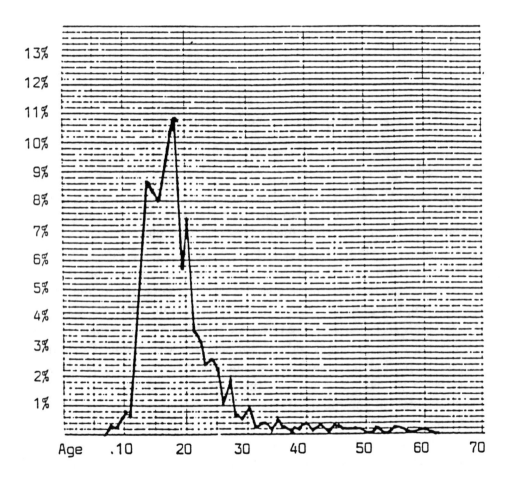

Figure 13. 4
Age Distribution of Respondents

The central tendency measures of *mode* and *median* for the age distribution are calculated in figure 13.5 with data broken down for Bangkok, Vicinity of Bangkok, and Provinces. (Mode is a measure of the highest number of responses, and Median is the middle answer.)

	Bangkok		Vicinity of Bangkok		Provinces	
	Men	Women	Men	Women	Men	Women
Mode	18	17	19	17,5	17	18
Median	19	18	19	18	18,5	17

Figure 13. 5
Age of Respondents and Geographical Location

For the interest of the reader, let us just mention that the data from this study was later compared with data from studies of other ministries using mail response. Students at two different correspondence courses had an average age of thirteen, and for a literature distribution organization the respondents had an average age of twelve. The data does, therefore, seem to indicate that we should not expect mail response from people above the age of thirty, and usually not above the age of twenty. These findings had obvious implications for other communication ministries, such as radio, where letters from listeners are often needed to establish contact. If a ministry broadcasts to a target audience of people above twenty-five years of age in this particular society, they should not expect letter responses, and, consequently, they have to base their contact-ministry (follow-up) on other channels of communication.

Geographic Distribution. It was expected that the majority of responses would come from the city of Bangkok. The data indicated that this was not the case. Approximately 70% came from the provinces, 24% from Bangkok, and 6% from the vicinity of Bangkok.

Sex of Respondents. One of the most surprising results of the analysis was that 63.9% of the responses came from men and only 36.1% from women. As the ads were placed in women's magazines an exploratory study was conducted in ten book shops to discover actual buyers and readers. This study confirmed that buyers and readers were primarily women.

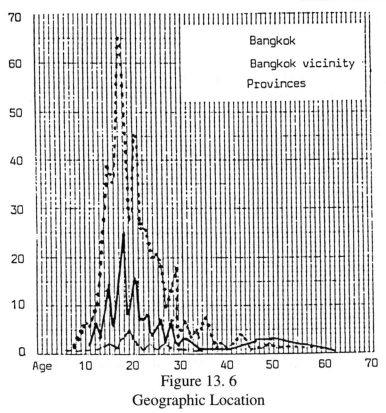

Figure 13. 6
Geographic Location

Male Responses	63.9%
Female Responses	36.1%

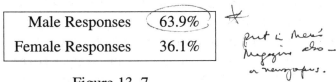

Figure 13. 7
Male-Female Distribution of Respondents

Recommendations to the Organization. The data indicated that the ads obviously attracted men more than women. It was therefore recommended that the organization place the ads in men's magazines, but for various reasons the organization did not feel comfortable with this suggestion. Instead, the second recommendation was followed and the ads were placed in newspapers, which are primarily read by men. Within one month, the response rate increased more than ten times for the same amount of money.

Further research should be conducted on second-time responses to get more accurate indicators of the effects of the ministry. The initial response, indicated by the coupons, could be just curiosity or an interest in getting something free through the mail.

Comments. This kind of research is, of course, crucial to any organization, but it needs to be augmented with actual audience research and testing prior to publication. This particular research project was, we could say, aimed at finding out where the "bullet" had hit and then draw a circle to indicate the target. On the other hand, if an organization is unaware of the composition of its present audience, such a study can be a first important step in the analysis and testing which eventually will lead to redefined purpose, objectives, and goal-oriented communication. It is also the kind of monitoring which all media enterprises could easily conduct as an ongoing evaluation. It was not an analysis of the present audience, but an analysis of those who responded to the ads by posting a response coupon. As such it provides us with information on possible use and effectiveness of a particular medium in a particular country at a particular time.

TESTING MEDIA PROGRAMS AND PRODUCTS

Copy is the technical word for the text in an ad. Usually, advertisers put a great deal of time and money into copy testing, where an ad will be tested at different phases of its development, from written concept to finished ad. A variety of methods can be used and secular advertising will spend considerable time and effort in testing an ad in controlled situations before placing it in the media.

By pretesting we mean field testing of materials and programs at various stages of production. Pretesting is always done among representatives of the intended audience with the aim of testing understanding and actual communication. Or, to ask questions such as, Is the program achieving its intended communication effects? Pretesting may also have to be repeated several times in order to see how changes have improved the relevancy of the programs.

In the following we will first briefly look at copy testing and then spend considerable space on pre-testing.

COPY TESTING METHODS

The following is a selection of copy-testing methods used by advertising agencies.

A **Consumer Jury** is a group of fifty to one hundred people from the target audience. They are interviewed either individually or in small groups. They may rank a set of ads in order of preference or some other perceived variable. We could, for example, test our listener's music tastes in a similar way.

In **Portfolio Tests** a group of people from the target audience is exposed to a package of both test and control ads, called a portfolio. Respondents are asked to look through the portfolio, reading whatever interests them. Book covers can be tested in a similar way, using a dummy sample.

Physiological Methods are among the more sophisticated measurement procedures. An eye camera can track the movement of the eye as it examines a picture or an ad, and a galvanic skin test can be used to measure physiological response. The tachistoscope is a slide projector with special capabilities that allows for the presentation of pictures or text under different levels of speed and illumination.

Inquiry Tests are used to measure the effectiveness of a message on the basis of either measured sales, or on inquiries received as a direct result of an ad or a special offer. It can be coupons returned from a magazine or newspaper.

On-the-Air Tests are used to give immediate information on actual listenership or viewers to television programs. The test is done when the program is actually on television or radio in test areas. Contacts are established by telephone and the respondents are asked which program they are watching or listening to. A few follow-up questions can be added.

Theater Tests. Television commercials are often tested in a theater environment. One such place is the Hollywood Preview House, where people are invited to attend a series of commercials and new programs. The audience is measured regarding brand preference, shifts based upon before and after exposure, and recall of specific points in the commercial. The approach can easily be adapted to measuring Christian media products and services.

Christian communicators can use all of these methods for testing media products. The main concern is not the number of methods used or how sophisticated the measurement techniques are, but the fact that our products are adequately tested before broadcasting or distribution.

PRETESTING

Before final production, all media programs, whether radio, audio cassettes or printed materials, should be tested thoroughly as to acceptability and understanding by the intended audience. Many former students and colleagues have said that pretesting procedures were the most important lessons they learned, and that it completely changed their ministries.

Some of the questions we seek to find answers to in pretesting would be:

Is the program to the likeness of the audience?
Are the symbols understood?
Is the language or dialect correct for this particular audience?
Will any part of it embarrass the reader/ listener/viewer?
Will what I am saying, or the way in which I say it cause offense among my non-Christian audience?

There is no reason for causing offense, even if the teaching is directed to Christians only. A non-Christian may also be listening, and then your program should be made in such a way that he or she will want to listen again.

Programs and various communication materials are usually developed by educated people living in urban areas, and often they do not know, or have forgotten, how rural people live and speak. And as producers are constantly working with their special topics, they tend to forget how other people respond to their messages. In many countries Christians are a minority, and they have developed their own subculture, and in doing so they have lost effective contact with the population at large. And the American televangelist who broadcasts copies of his US-based program in Nairobi or in Manila will not know the audience, or have even a faint idea about their felt needs. Careful evaluation and pretesting, even with the time and expenses involved, would in the long run prove to be much more cost-effective for the proclamation of the Kingdom of God.

Evaluation and pretesting are, then, cost-effective ways of reducing error or mistakes in programming. But, alas, most Christian organizations seem to be content with production of materials that are broadcast or published without such relevant testing. Some may conduct a limited amount of internal evaluation, but this cannot substitute for actual field testing or pretesting with the intended audience.

Why Some People Avoid Pretesting

There seems to be a number of problems and reasons which cause Christian organizations to avoid evaluation and pretesting procedures. A primary one is the sheer lack of knowledge and experience in pretesting. After all, few pastors pretest their messages. Another often quoted excuse is lack of time, as the tyranny of production schedules prevents producers from going into the field and testing their materials. A lot of lip-service will be given to the issue, though, but rarely do managers provide the time and expenses needed. In the secular world, it would be considered a waste of money and far too high a risk to take, if advertising is not well tested before it goes on the air or is published in a magazine.

Another underlying, but usually not expressed reason seems to be that people think they know how the audience will understand the material and respond to it. After all, a city person should have education enough to understand the villagers. But, we experience again and again that this is not so. And village people are sharp enough to understand this, and consequently screen out a radio program that might otherwise have helped them, or they laugh at the lifestyle of the actors in the video rather than listening to the message.[4]

Another reason is defensiveness on the part of the producers and artists. Unfortunately, they often understand evaluation and pretesting as criticism of "their" work and skills, but we then have to ask whether they are in the ministry for the sake of their art, or if they are in there to use such skills to communicate the gospel clearly to a needy world.

I do believe, though, that Christian leaders want their ministry to be effective, so let us trust that some day all Christian managers will take

---

4. Paul Hartmann et al., *The Mass Media and Village Life: An Indian Study.* University of Leister, 1983.

evaluation and pretesting as prerequisites and build it into production and distribution processes. It can be done so we need to work for adequate allocation of time and funds to see it happen.

Planning the Pretest

Pretesting is a multi-faceted task. It is a process of constantly monitoring both the production process and the actual communication process, so that we know how a particular program or series of programs perform in relation to its objectives. It covers the whole process: scripts should be tested, test-recordings should be made and evaluated, the final product should be tested before release, and finally a field test should be done to see if it really happened.

The timing of pretesting will therefore depend on a number of factors. If it is a new production, say a new type of radio program or a new set of flip charts, pretesting may be carried out at several stages, from the early draft to the finished program. A general suggestion would be to start the pretesting as early as you can in the process. A new radio program, using a magazine format, may, for example, be tested on both individual program segments and on the final, completed program. A book can be tested on its cover, layout, pictures, language, etc.

Respondents need to be representatives of the audience. It is often tempting to test the materials on friends and relatives who can learn the ideas quickly, or to go to those with a higher education. But such an approach is totally unacceptable unless the material is produced for them. We need to test with representatives of the intended or target audience.

Testing can be done with both individuals and groups, and there are a number of methods available for this. If you test with a group it is best to try to get the responses of individuals before group discussion in order to avoid biases by the most vocal members of the group.

The number of people in a pretest will vary, but usually a number around twenty will do, and sometimes even testing with just five people will give the necessary information. Ideally, you continue testing until you find a trend in the responses. After getting a fairly good idea of the necessary changes, you go back to the drawing board, re-write and re-produce, and then test again.

Generally speaking, pretesting is something all can do and many should be involved in: managers, producers, artists, writers, performers and others involved in the production, but the actual pretesting will often be directed by a researcher. In any case, it is always advisable to consult a researcher in setting up the test plan if it is to be done by those who are not trained in research. The artist or producer may feel tempted to defend their materials and not be objective in questioning, but it has been found that it is important for such workers to at least observe and listen to pretest interviews.[5]

A FEW GUIDELINES FOR ACTUAL PRETESTING

The following are practical guidelines for conducting personal pretests with individuals. These steps have proved to be helpful in successfully completing a pretest.

Get Cooperation to Conduct the Test

Pretesting is a communication situation and is therefore subject to all the principles of good interpersonal communication. In a community, it is necessary to obtain the necessary permission from the leaders of the community. In some places, other official permits are also required.

Sometimes pretesting will be a matter of asking a neighbor to help you look at some material. Often it is asking an individual directly to assist you in testing, at other times you need a group together. Very few people will refuse to help if you approach them nicely and ask them to help you improve a program.

Establish Rapport with the Respondent

Finding an appropriate place to conduct the pretest is often very important. Many people may want to listen or look on, but it is important that you establish good rapport with the respondent so that he or she does not feel inhibited by the social setting or context. Spend time talking with the

5. Ane Haaland, *Pretesting Communication Materials*. UNICEF, 1984.

person, especially if he or she is a stranger to you. The respondent needs to trust you with their time and insights and be willing to give critical remarks, if necessary. Another important point is that you should find a time that is convenient for the respondent so that the test can be carried out in a relaxed atmosphere. The purpose of the pretest should be carefully explained to the respondent and all encouragement should be given for him or her to make corrections or suggestions for change.

If an outside researcher is employed for the pretest, this person will need to be carefully briefed on the material being tested, its purpose and objectives. He or she will also need to study the audience and their previous experience with such material. Are they able to read and write? Is the topic one that they are familiar with? Would certain illustrations possibly be seen as threatening? Is the language or dialect of special importance?

Encourage Frank Responses

Always remember that you are testing programs and materials, not the people. Therefore, point this out clearly to the respondent and explain that there are no correct answers. All we need are their frank responses. Resist the temptation to teach or preach, even if the answers seem to call for that. If teaching or preaching is mixed with the pretest you will most likely get a biased evaluation of the material, and your attention will be drawn away from the actual purpose of the session.

Ask Questions

In asking questions, select unbiased questions. There may be a temptation to ask leading questions that will obtain a praise of the materials or programs, but such an approach will totally ruin the pretest, and in turn waste precious resources on poor productions that are not meeting needs.

Questions should be objective, calling for extended responses and not just "yes" or "no." In the pretest you can often use open-ended questions, and you will have to go into depth on certain issues. Be inquisitive, try to find out what the person really understands, how he or she feels about the program, interest in the topic, etc. One way of getting at sensitive issues is to ask: How do you think your neighbors would react to such a program?

Usually, the person will respond with his or her own perspective. When an answer or opinion is expressed, give a positive and friendly response, urging him or her to go on. Don't express any surprise at their answers.

The attitudes and behavior of the interviewers will usually greatly influence the responses. The person who usually gets the best and most useful information is the one who is really interested in the work and is keen on getting the reaction of people to the programs or materials being tested. He or she is concerned about making effective material and will therefore not be defensive. Analyze your attitudes to the people who are being interviewed. A lack of respect will be communicated in many subtle ways, but this will be understood by the respondents and their cooperation will be influenced. It is your attitudes that guide your behavior, your way of asking questions, your dress, your language and your responses. People will sense this and a negative attitude or lack of respect will alienate the respondent.

Record the Responses

For the purpose of analyzing the results of the pretest, it is important to have an accurate report of the questions as well as the answers. The answers may be recorded by either the interviewer or by an assistant. If the interviewer has to write down the answers, it may make the situation rather difficult and destroy a line of thought. One way is to use two people, one asking the questions and the other writing down the responses. In some cases, it may be possible to record the session on tape and transcribe the responses at a later time.

If the pretest is done in a group, it may be possible to have questionnaires that each individual fills out. In this way the anonymity of the person can be kept to encourage frank responses but it does, of course, presuppose that the pretest is done with people who are literate.

Analyze and Interpret the Responses

Pretesting is not like large research studies where variables have been clearly defined. It is therefore difficult to use a computer for analysis. The number is also small so the work involved is not sufficient to design special computer programs. Of course, in a wider testing with several groups and self-administered questionnaires, a computer may come in handy to analyze some of the responses and to identify trends.

Practical Exercise

It is recommended that the novice practice pretesting. The following exercise is designed for pretesting an audio cassette produced for Christians.

- *Contact a friend or neighbor, asking if he or she would mind helping you.* Tell them that you are working on this program and that you would like to be sure that it is helpful and does not offend anybody.
- *Bring the cassette to the person.* Ask him/her to listen and then tell you how they think others in the community would respond to it. Would they like it? Would they be offended? Would they understand? etc. You can be more or less sure that the person will be giving his or her own opinions, and you will be much wiser as a result.
- *Re-produce the segment* and if possible ask the same person to listen again.

EVALUATION PROCEDURES

In the section above, we have treated pretesting. Actually evaluation often comes before pretesting, or it is conducted during the same period of time. In this chapter we distinguish between pretesting and evaluation. Pretesting is with the intended audience. Evaluation is internal to the organization. There are several steps we will go through in our evaluation.

There may be an initial reaction against evaluation. Someone may say, I have worked hard on this, I have prayed for God's guidance, I know the message, why then should I "waste" time and money on evaluation? My colleagues have less experience than I have! The simple answer is that it is good stewardship, and it is a prerequisite for effective communication to carefully evaluate. If we do not evaluate, we may indeed be wasting money and time on producing materials that do not reach our intended audience in an effective way.

Self-Critique

The first phase in the evaluation process is your own self-critique. It is necessary to be hard on yourself when writing and producing a program.

The first step is to critique the script itself. A script will usually need to be rewritten. Good writers often rewrite their scripts several times. Go through the script, possibly using a felt pen, strike out unnecessary words and sentences. If this is a script for an audio medium, read it out loud for yourself to "feel" if it flows naturally and reads easily. If it is a script for a dramatic performance, try to "act" as you read through your script, making changes as needed.

For an audio program, the next step would be to record the message on tape. For the script writer, this can be done on a simple home cassette recorder. Then listen critically to the reading, and try to put yourself in the place of the intended listener. If you are a performer or speaker you will need a fairly good recording for such personal critique. As you listen, there may be several things with which you are not satisfied. Maybe the natural flow of the dialogue needs improvement. Try to ask some critical questions of yourself. Here are a few suggestions:

1. Did the voice sound natural, like talking to a friend?
2. Was it happy enough to make the listener smile a little?
3. Did the program have an interesting beginning?
4. Would the program be interesting to my listener?
5. Was the reading or talk the right length?
6. Did it sound believable and trustworthy?
7. Were the words simple enough for my listener?
8. Did it deal with issues that my listener would find important?

If the program is for a visual medium such as television or video, or even if it is for a personal delivery such as a speech, you may want to have a preliminary video recording to see how you perform and how the message comes together as it is translated through both sound and visuals. You can, of course, also do some practicing in front of a mirror.

Good self-critique before going into further evaluation with colleagues will save time for all concerned, and you will be more ready to listen to the advice from other members on the team.

Internal Evaluation

The next phase is the internal evaluation by your own colleagues or staff. For this purpose it is helpful to have an evaluation form which people can fill out as they listen. Usually a five-point scale is adequate for judging the response. The actual number of issues on the form can be increased or decreased as needed for your particular program. The form shown in figure 13.7 can be used for the internal evaluation of an audio cassette.

	Bad (1)	Poor (2)	Acceptable (3)	Good (4)	Excellent (5)
1. Interesting					
2. Understandable					
3. Credible					
4. Relevant topic					
5. Appropriate voices					
6. Friendly					
7. Music selection					
8. Spoken language					
9. Program format					
10. Sound effects					
11. Recording quality					
12.					
13.					

Figure 13. 7
Internal Evaluation

If you were evaluating a sermon, you would include topics such as gestures and facial expressions, eye contact with the congregation, dress, etc. Evaluation of a slide-tape presentation would include questions related to the pictures themselves, such as the selection of pictures and the speed of presentation.

How to Conduct Evaluation in a Group Setting

It has been found that internal evaluation should, if possible, take place in a group setting. If done individually, people tend to be either too nice, and consequently not helpful in the evaluation, or the comments are accepted as criticism rather than critique. Criticism is negative and destructive, critique can be both negative and positive and its purpose is to provide help for improvement.

If public speaking or some kind of performance is involved, record the presentation on video, and then let the speaker or performer see the playback before any discussion takes place. Then, let everybody fill out a form individually prior to group discussion. A form may also be shown on the board for recording the average responses. Finally, discussion will follow, aimed at both highlighting positive strengths of the talk or program and identifying weaknesses.

If possible, make evaluation a regular event, maybe a session every week or two. At one radio organization, a weekly session was conducted and the producers took turns in presenting a program. Some other members of staff also attended the sessions, and they found that such an internal evaluation exercise heightened quality far more than many seminars and workshops. The "agenda" for the evaluation session was:

---

1. *The producer explains intended audience, program goal, and how such effects can be observed or tested.*
2. *All present are given an evaluation form.*
3. *Listen to program.*
4. *All fill out form prior to any discussion.*
5. *The producer gives his or her comments.*
6. *Scores given by all present are averaged and put on the board.*
7. *Discussion of the results, highlight weaknesses, and make suggestions for improvement.*

Figure 13. 8
Program Agenda for Evaluation Session

As a staff, develop a form that will fit your particular ministry, a form that reflects your needs for evaluation, and of which you as a staff feel ownership. Then make it a point to have a regular evaluation session, if possible weekly. Regularity is important in order to develop an evaluation thinking and to secure long-term effects.

14

SHALOM AS A MEASURE OF MINISTRY

The following is a case study which is presented here to illustrate the development of a measuring system for an organization with a specific need. The project will illustrate the various steps that we often need to go through to arrive at appropriate measuring systems.

WORLD VISION CONTEXT

World Vision International is committed to communicating the values of the kingdom of God as an integrated part of its holistic ministry. Most of the methods used by Christian organizations seem to be designed to work among those people groups which are to some degree open to the gospel and which have some limited knowledge of what the Christian religion is about. There seems to be few methods that are appropriate for use among people groups who are resistant to the gospel or who have no knowledge of Christianity at all.

But, World Vision is working extensively in such contexts, and there existed, therefore, a need to develop a range of indicators to measure evangelistic effects of development ministries. The tendency to rely on numbers of conversions or new church members would not suffice among people groups where resistance to the gospel is high and knowledge is low. The impact of ministry may not lead to conversion. However, it may significantly lessen the resistance and increase the knowledge, thus setting

233

the stage for successful proclamation by someone else in the future. Unless we could develop measurable indicators for ministry effects, we might be led to believe that there had been no evangelistic impact at all. The reverse could also be true, so there is a need to have measures which show if our contribution has in fact been positive, rather than one which raises resistance or presents a negative caricature of the gospel.

The need was then to develop standards and measurable indicators for evangelistic effects. The information obtained could then be applied to strategy development in the diversified cultural contexts in which the organization worked. Each situation may call for different approaches and possibly different measures of effectiveness.

Approach to Ministry

In order to understand the needed measuring system, we need to understand the basic philosophy of the organization. The World Vision approach to development ministry is based on an understanding that "the end does *not* justify the means," but that the approach itself and the means used are in themselves characteristic attributes of the desired results. These characteristics reflect an understanding of the *constants* in Christian ministry and communication. Christian communication is unique in relation to other forms of communication due to the fact that we operate within a set of constant factors that permeate all our ministry and characterize our approaches. An exhaustive treatment of such factors cannot be given here, but some of the most important issues are: (1) the awareness of the ever presence and revelation of God, (2) the supernatural nature of the work and the role of the Spirit, (3) the involvement of Christians as facilitators of ministry, (4) the presence and activity of the powers of darkness, (5) the authority of the Word of God, and (6) the ever-present commission of disciple-making.

At the same time, there is also an awareness of the variable factors that govern our approach and Christian communication. Some of these variables are: (1) a respect for the cultural context of the people served, (2) an understanding of the specific society in which they live, (3) a knowledge of the spiritual position of the people, and (4) the acceptance of the fact the Christian communicators have a variety of gifts and skills.

When analyzing the impact of World Vision in a given area, it is important to assess how well the ministry has paid attention to such factors. It presupposes that a project is in itself both a channel of communication and an "evangelistic" activity, but such activities are seen as integrated in the project itself and may in themselves be of less significance than the lifestyle of the staff and the approach to ministry exemplified by the project. This, in turn, makes significant demands on World Vision strategy development, as each project must be planned from such an integrated perspective.

DEVELOPMENT OF RESEARCH MEASURES

There is a tendency to confuse a research plan with the actual ministry. Research will never measure everything, but only selected variables. Earlier in this book an illustration was given of a visit to a medical clinic. A medical doctor diagnoses a sickness based on certain tests, so a researcher will select tests on which to base recommendations. The sophistication of the measuring apparatus will, of course, influence the accuracy of the diagnosis. A doctor with x-ray, lab tests, etc. will be in a better position to make an accurate diagnosis and prescribe the correct treatment than a village health worker with only a thermometer. The task for a Christian development agency is both to use the "doctor" and the village "health worker" and provide both of them with necessary tools of measurement. Our problem was that neither the measurements nor the instruments were readily available for measuring evangelistic effects of holistic ministry. Basic research was needed to make such information and tools available.

It is realized that the measuring of holistic effects is an extremely difficult task and must be treated with utmost care and skill. We are primarily concerned with lifestyle and psychographics (which is the operational measure of lifestyle, providing quantitative measures). We will need to use nominal data that deal with constructs in people's minds. The challenge is to isolate measurable variables, or indicators that will give us valid information on which causal statements can be made.

RESEARCH OF HOLISTIC MINISTRY IN SHALOM PERSPECTIVE

As mentioned above, research cannot measure everything, but we must attempt, on the basis of an accepted conceptual framework, to measure certain selected points. Initially, this present study attempted to isolate such variables by starting at the applied area, but we soon ran into numerous snags as we had hundreds of possible "indicators" on our hands. We needed, first of all, to develop the conceptual framework, and then proceed with the development of applied research instruments.

We have, in the following proposal, used the framework of *shalom*, interpreted as the reign of right relationships.[1] This has provided us with a matrix in which we can *measure progress towards Kingdom Values* by the *participants*. The matrix follows general research methodological principles by analyzing cognitive, affective and behavioral effects.

	Relationship with God	Relationship with Self	Relationship with Others	Relationship with Creation	Relationship with Church
Cognitive	What they know about God	What they know about Self	What they know about Others	What they know about Creation	What they know about Church
Affective	How they feel towards God	How they feel towards Self	How they feel towards Others	How they feel towards Creation	How they feel towards Church
Behavioral	How they act towards God	How they act towards Self	How they act towards Others	How they act towards Creation	How they act towards Church

Figure 14. 1
Shalom as Basis for Research

Standards of Ministry

For each of the *squares* of the matrix, a *standard* was necessary so that we had a goal towards which our measures could be directed. We could also call this the ultimate goal, or God's intended future. The matrix in figure

1. William A. Dyrness, *Let the Earth Rejoice, A Biblical Theology of Holistic Mission.* Fuller Seminary Press, 1983.

14.2 is presented as an initial proposal that probably needs further refining and improvement. A scriptural base was also developed for each *standard*. The column Relationship with Church in figure 14.1 was added at a later stage and is therefore not included in all of the following material.

	Relationship with God	**Relationship with Self**	**Relationship with Others**	**Relationship with Creation**
Cognitive	(1) People understand they are created for relationship with God	(4) People realize meaning of being created in the image of God	(7) People recognize others as created in the image of God	(10) People are stewards of God's abundance resources of creation
Affective	(2) People enjoy communion with God	(5) People value themselves as God values them	(8) People esteem others as God sees them	(11) People feel responsible for wise use and preservation of nature's resources
Behavioral	(3) People communicate with God	(6) People demonstrate responsible actions as image bearers	(9) People act in love towards neighbors	(12) People participate in maintaining, enhancing and developing nature's resources

Figure 14. 2
Standards for Holistic Measures

Indicators

The *standards* given in figure 14.2 cannot be directly observed or measured. Measurable *indicators* were, therefore, identified. *Indicators* are carefully selected, as it is on the basis of such indicators we make our decisions regarding a person's or a group's position in the process. The standards can be developed for universal use, but indicators may need to be based on the specific socio-cultural context of the people. On the chart in figure 14.3, three indicators are selected for each standard. The selection of these particular indicators was based on extensive work by staff groups in India and in the Philippines. The reader will obviously notice the World Vision context.

	Relationship with God	Relationship with Self	Relationship with Others	Relationship with Creation
Cognitive	(1) People understand they are created for relationship with God *Indicators*: 1. Knows the reality of the living God 2. Knows sin disrupted relationship with God 3. Knows Christ restores relationship with God	(4) People realize meaning of being created in the image of God *Indicators*: 1. Knows the account of creation of humanity 2. Knows God's view of human beings 3. Knows his/her own worth	(7) People recognize others as created in the image of God *Indicators*: 1. Knows scriptural view of equality of people 2. Knows Jesus' identity with the poor and lonely 3. Knows the God-given potentialities of all people	(10) People are stewards of God's abundant resources of creation *Indicators*: 1. Understands God owns nature's resources 2. Knows God has made us stewards of creation 3. Understands nature's resources are for all to enjoy
Affective	(2) People enjoy communion with God *Indicators*: 1. Belief in God 2. Peace with God 3. Love for God	(5) People value themselves as God values them *Indicators*: 1. Possesses self-esteem 2. Manifests inner freedom 3. Displays confidence concerning the future	(8) People esteem others as God sees them *Indicators*: 1. Regards others as important 2. Likes to fellowship with others 3. Wants to build up others	(11) People feel responsible for wise use and preservation of nature's resources *Indicators*: 1. Feels awed by nature's beauty and worth 2. Feels indignant towards destructive exploitation 3. Feels honored to be creation's stewards
Behavioral	(3) People communicate with God *Indicators*: 1. Meditates on the Word of God and prays 2. Participates in worship 3. Behaves according to God's character	(6) People demonstrate responsible actions as image bearers *Indicators*: 1. Cares for the body 2. Enhancement of the mind 3. Development of the spirit	(9) People act in love towards neighbors *Indicators*: 1. Identifies with the poor 2. Assists in meeting the basic needs of the poor 3. Defends the rights of the poor	(12) People participate in maintaining, enhancing and developing nature's resources *Indicators*: 1. Gets involved in the preservation of resources 2. Develops nature's resources 3. Assists in proper sharing of nature's resources

Figure 14. 3
Standards and Indicators

Each Indicator is a Process

For each of these indicators, we need a continuum for the purpose of constructing research instruments. The steps in the continuum need to reflect a natural progress. All choices need to be mutually exclusive, but at the same time inclusive of all possible positions. The following *scale* was developed as an illustration of how the results might look for indicator number 9.1 on the matrix, "Identifies with the poor." It reflects the specific need of World Vision as they work primarily among very poor people, and this particular example is more directed at the staff than at the people being served.

1. Exploitation of the poor.
2. Avoidance of the poor.
3. Try to understand but remain passive.
4. Contact with the poor.
5. Acceptance by the poor.
6. Complete integration with the poor.

Research Measurements and Instruments

The actual instrument for data collection still needs further refinement to assure reliability. The draft questionnaire at the end of this chapter should therefore be understood as a form to be used in further testing of the instrument itself. On this particular questionnaire, questions regarding relationship with the church have been included.

A decision was made to use only four steps in the process rather than a higher number as indicated by the example above. For some questions, it would have been desirable to have a higher number of steps, but for ease in tabulation and to provide cohesiveness to the instrument, it was decided to use only four steps for all questions. Also, on a "final" questionnaire that will be used in actual field situations, the answers will be scrambled so that the respondent cannot see from the questionnaire itself which answer is the "best one," or try to imagine which answer the interviewer would like to have.

Presenting the Results

Results obtained by the questionnaire can be tabulated and presented on a graph as the one presented in figure 14.4. There are three measures for each topic, and as each measure can give a total of 3 "points," the combined value of a topic can be illustrated on a continuum from 0 to 9. On the following graph, some imagined results have been recorded as an illustration.

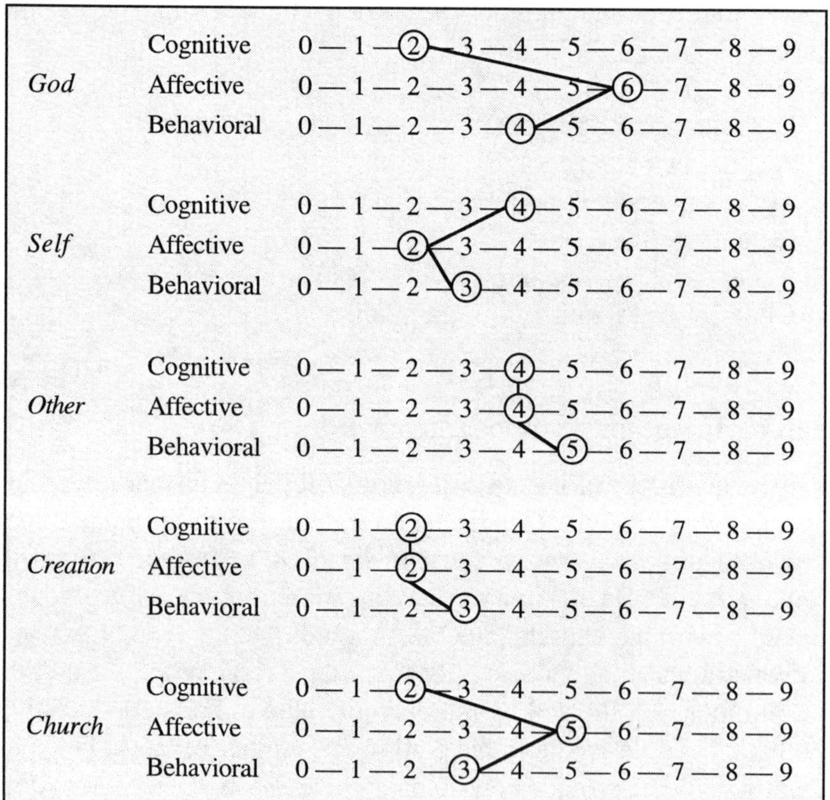

Figure 14. 4
Presenting the Results

(Measuring Holistic Ministry in the Perspective of Shalom)

DRAFT QUESTIONNAIRE (UNSCRAMBLED)

Please select the answer to each question that would be closest to your personal answer.

1. **What is your understanding of who God is?**
   (1) __ I don't know if there is a God.
   (2) __ I believe God exists but I don't know much about Him.
   (3) __ I know God was the creator of the universe.
   (4) __ I believe that God is living and active in our daily lives.

2. **How do you understand the word sin?**
   (1) __ I don't know what sin is.
   (2) __ I know that I am a sinner.
   (3) __ I know that sin separates us from God.
   (4) __ I know that God forgives my sin when I confess and repent of my sin.

3. **What is the relationship between sin and Jesus Christ?**
   (1) __ I don't know of any relationship.
   (2) __ Jesus died on the cross for sin.
   (3) __ Jesus is the mediator between man and God.
   (4) __ Jesus makes a personal relationship between me and God possible

4. **How would you describe your belief in God?**
   (1) __ I do not believe in God.
   (2) __ I feel that I may need God.
   (3) __ I believe in God.
   (4) __ I put my trust in God every day.

5. **How would you describe your relationship with God?**
   (1) __ I don't know God.
   (2) __ Sometimes I feel need for peace with God.
   (3) __ I have at one time repented and prayed for God's peace in my heart.
   (4) __ I am enjoying peace and harmony with God.

6. How do you feel about God?
- (1) __ I don't really believe there is a God.
- (2) __ I don't feel anything special about God.
- (3) __ I often long for experiencing God's love.
- (4) __ I love God and He loves me.

7. How much time do you spend on reading or listening to the Bible?
- (1) __ I never read or listen to the Bible.
- (2) __ I sometimes read or listen to the Bible.
- (3) __ I attend some Bible studies.
- (4) __ I regularly read or listen to the Bible.

8. How often do you attend church?
- (1) __ I never attend church activities.
- (2) __ I go to church occasionally.
- (3) __ I attend church regularly.
- (4) __ I take part in church worship and other church activities.

9. How would you describe your Christian lifestyle?
- (1) __ I don't care much about my lifestyle.
- (2) __ I don not know what Christian life is.
- (3) __ I make some attempts at living as a Christian.
- (4) __ I try to conform to Christian lifestyle.

10. What do you believe about the creation of the human race?
- (1) __ I believe mankind came into being through an evolutionary process.
- (2) __ I know little about the creation of the human race.
- (3) __ I am well acquainted with the biblical story about the creation of man.
- (4) __ I believe God created man to be in charge of the rest of creation.

11. How does God look at human beings?
- (1) __ There is no relation between God and human beings.
- (2) __ I don't really know how God looks at people.
- (3) __ People are created in the image of God.
- (4) __ God places high value on the human beings he created.

12. How do you look at yourself?
(1) __ I don't think much of myself.
(2) __ I think that I have some value in God's sight.
(3) __ I know God has given me some potentials.
(4) __ I can use my gifts to help others.

13. How do you feel about yourself?
(1) __ I don't care much about myself.
(2) __ I don't really like the way I am.
(3) __ I feel okay about the way I am.
(4) __ I am happy for the way God made me.

14. Do you feel that you are personally free?
(1) __ I don't feel any need for freedom.
(2) __ I often feel that I am not really free.
(3) __ I often feel constrained by legalism.
(4) __ I enjoy freedom and feel that I am free.

15. What do you think of the future?
(1) __ I don't really care about the future.
(2) __ I believe the future is going to be worse.
(3) __ I am uncertain about what happens in the future.
(4) __ I am confident that God will be with me in the future.

16. How do you treat your body?
(1) __ I don't do anything about it.
(2) __ I really neglect looking after my body.
(3) __ When I am sick, I take medicine.
(4) __ I try to take good care of my body.

17. Are you involved in any educational program?
(1) __ I don't think about education.
(2) __ I don't really participate in given opportunities.
(3) __ Sometimes I attend a training course.
(4) __ I do what I can to improve my education and skills.

18. How do you develop your spiritual life?

(1) __ I don't really do anything.

(2) __ Once in a while I attend worship service.

(3) __ I have regular devotions on my own.

(4) __ I try to follow Christ in my daily life.

19. Do you think all people are equal?

(1) __ I do not believe in this talk about equality.

(2) __ I do not know what the Bible says about equality of people.

(3) __ I am uncertain about equality of people.

(4) __ I believe in the equality of people.

20. How did Jesus treat the poor?

(1) __ I don't know if Jesus had any special concern for the poor.

(2) __ Jesus gave priority to the poor.

(3) __ Jesus identified with the poor.

(4) __ Jesus gave me an example of how I should treat the poor.

21. Have all people been given possibilities?

(1) __ No, only some have potential for development.

(2) __ I don't know if God has given same potential to all.

(3) __ Everybody has some God-given potential.

(4) __ I try to discover and develop the potential in others.

22. How do you feel about other people?

(1) __ I don't really care about others.

(2) __ I let other people take care of themselves.

(3) __ I try to look up to other people.

(4) __ I am happy when others are doing well.

23. How would you describe your interest in having relationship with other people?

(1) __ I don't want any close relationships with others.

(2) __ I do not feel any need for developing personal relationships.

(3) __ I'm quite happy to have some fellowship with other people.

(4) __ I consciously try to develop close personal relationship with others.

24. How strong is your desire for helping other people?

(1) __ I don't really do anything to help others.

(2) __ I sometimes try to encourage helping people in need.

(3) __ I want other people to succeed.

(4) __ I like to be involved in helping others.

25. What is your relationship with the poor?

(1) __ I don't have any relationship with the poor.

(2) __ I don't think much about the poor.

(3) __ I'm in regular contact with poor people.

(4) __ I feel accepted by the poor.

26. How do you reach to the needs of the poor?

(1) __ I treat them as other people do.

(2) __ I don't do much to meet the needs of the poor.

(3) __ I give some of my wealth to the poor.

(4) __ I am involved in helping the poor develop.

27. What is your position on the rights of the poor?

(1) __ They need to fight for their own rights.

(2) __ I don't deal with the issue of the rights of the poor.

(3) __ I try to speak on behalf of the poor.

(4) __ I work for the rights of the poor.

28. How do you understand God's relationship to this world?

(1) __ For me there is no relationship.

(2) __ I don't know if there is a relationship.

(3) __ God created the universe.

(4) __ As creator He is the owner of the earth.

29. As people, what kind of responsibility do we have for nature's resources?

(1) __ This is not our responsibility.

(2) __ I am not aware of any responsibility.

(3) __ I understand that God made mankind stewards of resources.

(4) __ We are responsible for wise use of nature's resources.

30. How should nature's resources be distributed?

(1) __ Every person should look after himself.

(2) __ I don't think there is enough for everyone.

(3) __ God's intention was to provide for everyone.

(4) __ I believe that nature's resources should be available for all to enjoy.

31. How do you feel about the beauty and worth of nature?

(1) __ I never think about nature's beauty and worth.

(2) __ I don't let it influence my actions.

(3) __ I realize that nature is beautiful.

(4) __ I rejoice in the beauty and worth of nature.

32. How do you feel about nature being exploited?

(1) __ Some exploitation is necessary.

(2) __ I don't feel good about the exploitation that is going on.

(3) __ I am offended by the way nature's resources are exploited.

(4) __ I would like to participate in the preservation of nature's resources.

33. Do you feel any personal responsibility for creation?

(1) __ No, I am not personally responsible.

(2) __ I sense a certain responsibility.

(3) __ Yes, I am also responsible.

(4) __ I want all of us to be good stewards of the created universe.

34. What are you doing with nature's resources?

(1) __ I'm just using them.

(2) __ I let others use resources as they want.

(3) __ I am involved in some preventive measures for the preservation of nature's resources.

(4) __ I am campaigning for others to be involved in preservation of nature's resources.

35. Are you involved in developing new resources?

(1) __ No, I'm just using present resources.

(2) __ I let others take care of this.

(3) __ I try to develop nature's resources for personal use.

(4) __ I participate in restoring and developing nature's resources.

36. Are you actively involved in the sharing of nature's resources?

(1) __ I don't share with others.

(2) __ I allow others to fight for themselves.

(3) __ I give some help to others.

(4) __ I work for just distribution of nature's resources.

37. How do you understand the church?

(1) __ I don't really know what the Bible teaches about the church.

(2) __ I know that the church has some role to play.

(3) __ I know it's necessary for believers to come together.

(4) __ The church is the body of Christ.

38. What is the relationship between the church and the Kingdom of God?

(1) __ I don't think there is any relationship.

(2) __ There may be some relationship but I cannot explain it.

(3) __ The church is a visible sign of God's presence.

(4) __ The church demonstrates the Kingdom through its ministry.

39. What do you see is the role of the church?

(1) __ I don't see the church having a role in the world.

(2) __ The church is indifferent to the needs of the world.

(3) __ The church should be a servant.

(4) __ Christ has made the church responsible for demonstrating the Kingdom of God.

40. How do you feel about the local church?

(1) __ I am not attracted by the local church.

(2) __ I don't want to be involved in the local church.

(3) __ I know the local church needs my involvement.

(4) __ I am part of the local church.

41. How do you feel your relationship is with the local believers?

(1) __ I feel that I don't belong to them.

(2) __ Maybe I should have fellowship with local believers.

(3) __ I would like to be one with the local believers.

(4) __ I feel I am one of them.

42. Do you experience fulfillment in service with the local church?

(1) __ No, I seek such fulfillment in other places.

(2) __ I do not receive spiritual satisfaction in the local church.

(3) __ Yes, I am enriched by the local church.

(4) __ I get fulfillment by serving with the local church.

43. How often do you attend the local church?

(1) __ I don't really go there.

(2) __ I attend occasionally.

(3) __ I attend services on Sundays.

(4) __ I take part in the ministry of the local church.

44. Do you use your spiritual gifts in the local church?

(1) __ I don't participate in the local church.

(2) __ There is no scope for that in the local church.

(3) __ I'm trying to do it.

(4) __ Yes, I am meaningfully involved.

45. Do you participate in witnessing together with the local church?

(1) __ No, I am not involved.

(2) __ I do not see this as my calling.

(3) __ Now and then I participate.

(4) __ I participate regularly in witnessing with the local church.

15

GLOSSARY OF RESEARCH TERMS

Acquired source: A source which has supplied data obtained from an original or primary source.

Affective component: One of three main components of attitudes which relates to a person's feelings regarding an object or phenomenon.

Aided recall: A survey technique where the respondent is given cues regarding the topic of interest.

AIO Questions: Used to analyze lifestyle through questions related to activities, interests, and opinions.

Analysis of variance (ANOVA): A method primarily used in experiments when dealing with both an intervally-scaled dependent variable and one or more nominally-scaled independent variables.

Applied research: Research that is carried out with the specific purpose of providing information for decision-making.

Area sampling: A form of cluster sampling where only certain geographic areas are selected.

Attitude: An individual's evaluative position in respect of an object, a person, or a phenomenon.

Attitude scaling: A variety of measurement scales used to measure attitudes.

Audimeter: A mechanical device used by rating organizations to record when a television set is on and to which channel it is tuned.

Average: A term used for central tendency related to the terms mean, mode, and medium.

Bar chart: A graphic presentation of data where the data set is illustrated by the length of the bars.

Basic research: A research project that aims at expanding theory and knowledge regarding some topic or phenomenon.

Behavioral component: One of three main components of attitudes which relates to a person's behavior or response regarding an object or phenomenon.

Bias: Inaccuracy in survey data resulting from faulty steps in the research design process, including misleading questions.

Bipolar adjectives: A pair of adjectives used to define opposite ends of a continuum as in a semantic differential scale.

Cartoon completion: A questioning technique where the respondent is shown a cartoon drawing of a certain situation and then asked to complete a cartoon in response to a question.

Case: A unit of analysis. Usually each survey respondent is a case.

Causal research: Conclusive research designed to study cause-and-effect relationships.

Census: A study in which all members of a population are surveyed.

Central tendency measures: A type of descriptive statistics to arrive at averages, including the use of mean, median, and mode.

Chi-square test: A statistical procedure to test whether differences between two or more sets of data are due to chance variations.

Close-ended question: A question on a questionnaire with structured answers.

Cluster sampling: A sampling method where respondents are randomly selected from clusters or groups of respondents.

Coding: The assignment of numbers to responses on a questionnaire in order to establish categories for computer entry.

Cognitive component: One of three main components of attitudes, concerned with a person's knowledge about some object or phenomenon.

Communication method: The method used for collecting data from respondents, either verbally or by means of written questionnaires.

Computer card: A card with eighty columns used to punch in data for computer analysis.

Computer graphics: The display of research data in the form of graphics such as pie charts, bar graphs, and line charts.

Conclusive research: Research designed to assist in evaluating different courses of action and selecting the best one.

Concurrent validity: A method used to assess validity by having different questions relating to the same phenomena.

Confidence interval: The area of estimated values of the sample within which the true value falls with a predetermined probability.

Construct validity: The extent to which a measure corresponds to the underlying theoretical rationale.

Consumer jury: A representative group of consumers selected for ongoing pretesting purposes.

Content validity: The appropriateness of a given measure as subjectively assessed by an expert.

Contrived observation: A technique used in experimental research where the behavior of persons are observed in a created environment.

Control markets: The testing of products and services in a limited geographical area or within a limited context.

Convenience sample: The selection of a sample on the basis of the convenience of the researcher.

Correlation coefficient, *r*: A bivariate descriptive statistic, appropriate when dealing with two intervally-scaled variables.

Cross-sectional design: As compared to a longitudinal research, a cross-sectional research design involves taking a sample of population elements at one point in time.

Cross-tabulation: Comparing data from subgroups to determine variations in responses to important questions.

Data: The observations and responses gathered from respondents in a research project.

Data deck: A complete set of computer cards containing all the data from a given research project.

Data matrix: A data list where rows correspond to cases and columns to the individual variables or questions.

Decision criteria: The rules developed prior to a research project for selecting courses of action or application of research findings.

Decision problem: A situation in which a decision has to be reached, but two or more alternative courses of action exist.

Degrees of freedom: A formula to determine if data analyzed by a chi square test is statistically significant. The formula is *rows minus one multiplied by columns minus one ((r-1)(c-1))*.

Demographic information: The classification of data based on such information as age, education, income, job, and church membership.

Dependent variable: The variable that is presumed to have been influenced and an effect caused.

Depth interview: A personal interview where the interviewer can use extensive probing and follow-up questions to obtain details from a respondent.

Descriptive research: A survey research project aimed at describing a situation at a given point in time.

Descriptive statistics: Statistical methods that provide summary measures for the data in a samples.

Diary method: A method where respondents make written reports over a period of time, usually related to television viewing behavior.

Dichotomous question: A question on a questionnaire where the respondent is provided with only two choices like *yes* or *no*.

Disguised observation: An observation technique where the respondents are not aware that they are being observed.

Dummy advertising: A method used in pretesting where test and control ads are inserted into a magazine format. Respondents are asked to read the magazine and then respond to a set of questions.

Editing: The process of evaluating completed questionnaires to ensure that they have been filled out according to instructions. It will seek to ensure maximum accuracy and minimal ambiguity; check responses for legibility, consistency, and completeness.

Element: The basic unit in a sample about which we seek information.

Error: A statistical term describing the extent to which data collected through sampling fails to reflect the true data in the population or universe.

Experiment: A research process in which all things are held constant while one or more factors are varied systematically to reveal the effects of these variations.

Exploratory research: Research designed to explore a situation and find possible opportunities or potential problems, often used prior to a major survey research project to establish parameters for structured questions.

External validity: The degree to which the results of a research study is generalizable to other situations.

Field operation: The phase of a research project where interviewers conduct the actual interviews with respondents.

Focus group interview: A small number of respondents are interviewed simultaneously by a trained moderator.

Forced scale: A rating scale where respondents are requested to indicate a position on the attitude scale. It does not include a "no opinion" or "no knowledge" answer possibility.

Hypothesis: A tentative statement that generalizes a relationship between two or more variables and as such predicts a research or experimental outcome.

Incentive: Some form of inducement to encourage response to a questionnaire.

Independent variable: The variable that is presumed to have been the cause in a cause-and-effect relationship.

Indirect observation: An observation technique where records of past behavior are used to predict present behavior.

Indirect scale: Several questions are combined in order to develop a measure of a person's position or attitude to a certain topic.

Information: Data from a study that has been interpreted in relation to a specific decision need.

Inquiry tests: Analysis of actual responses, either from direct sales or from some other kind of inquiries or feedback.

Internal data: Data that is already available within the organization for which research is being conducted.

Internal validity: The extent to which combined experimental results are based on expected conditions rather than on extraneous variables.

Interval scale: A scale of measurement where intervals between numbers are assumed to be equal.

Judgment sample: A sample that is selected on the basis of the judgment by an expert who understands the context of the study.

Likert scale: A questioning method where the respondent is asked to indicate his or her degree of agreement or disagreement with a series of statements.

Line chart: A line chart is a graphical presentation of data by a line on a two-dimensional chart.

Longitudinal design: A research design where the same phenomenon or group of people are studied over a period of time.

Marketing information system (MIS): A systematic and continuous system for gathering, analyzing, and reporting data for decision-making purposes.

Marketing research: The application of research methodology to the development and provision of information for marketing decisions.

Mean: A measurement used to arrive at central tendency for interval data, usually called the average.

Measurement: The assignment of numbers to characteristics of objects or events according to certain rules.

Measures of dispersion: Descriptive statistics such as the standard deviation, coefficient of variation, interquartile range, and relative and absolute frequencies.

Mechanical observation: Research techniques involving mechanical observations or measurements such as a video camera.

Median: The "middle" score when data is arranged in order of magnitude. A measure of central tendency for ordinal data.

Mode: A measure of central tendency for nominal data, defined as the score that occurs most often in a frequency distribution.

Multiple-choice question: A question on a questionnaire where the respondent is asked to select an answer from among a list of possible answers.

Multivariate analysis: A method where more than two variables are analyzed at a time.

Nominal scale: A measurement scale in which numbers serve only as labels to identify or categorize objects or events.

Nonprobability sampling: A sampling procedure in which the sample is not based on any form of randomness, but on the judgment of the researcher or field interviewer.

Nonresponse error: Error that has been caused by those who do not respond to a questionnaire or a question.

Nonsampling errors: All the errors that may occur in a research process, but which is not due to sampling error.

Null hypothesis: The denial or negation of a research hypothesis.

Observation method: A nonobtrusive method where information is gathered without the use of a questionnaire or direct interaction with a respondent.

Omnibus panel: A fixed sample of respondents that are used for a variety of measures. Usually, the sample is contacted several times.

On-the-air tests: Research conducted at the same time as a certain radio or television program is actually on the air. The research is usually done by phone.

Open-ended question: A question where respondents are asked to provide their own answers on a blank line.

Ordinal scale: A scale of measurement where respondents are asked to rank items along a continuum.

Original source: The source from which data was originally obtained.

Parameter: A summary description or characteristic of a population.

Performance-monitoring research: Ongoing research that monitors results.

Pie chart: A graphical presentation of data where a circle is divided into sections, and the size of each section corresponds to a portion of the total findings.

Population: The target group from which the sample is selected. Another term is universe.

Portfolio tests: An approach used in pretesting ads where respondents are presented with a package of control and test ads.

Posttesting: An evaluation of a program after it has run in the media, or of an activity after it has taken place.

Pretesting: Trial use of a questionnaire on a small number of people to verify that questions communicate as intended and are correctly understood.

Probability sampling: A sampling procedure designed in such a way that each element of the population has a known chance of being selected for the sample.

Profile analysis: A method used to analyze data obtained on a semantic differential scale. The arithmetic mean or median is calculated for each set of polar opposites.

Proportionate stratified sampling: A stratified sample in which the number of elements drawn from each stratum is proportionate to the relative number of elements in each stratum of the population.

Psychographic research: A term used for analysis of lifestyle through questions on activities, interests, and opinions.

Purposive sample: A nonrandom sampling method in which individuals or groups are chosen through the judgment of the researcher as being representative of the population.

Qualitative research: A nonnumerical study and evaluation of observations aimed at understanding underlying dynamics.

Quantitative research: A research study requiring the measurement of variables. It is usually done on a large sample.

Questionnaire: A structured form used for collecting data from respondents.

Quota sample: A nonrandom sample selected by the researcher on the basis of some prespecified characteristics such as age and gender.

Random error: Bias in the measurements caused by factors not controlled by the researcher.

Random sample: Like a probability sample where each respondent has a known and equal chance of being selected.

Rank-order scale: A self-reporting technique in which the respondent ranks various objects on a continuum.

Rating scale: A self-reporting method where respondents are asked to indicate their responses on a verbal or graphic rating scale.

Ratio scale: A scale of measurement with an absolute zero point.

Recall tests: A posttesting method used to test respondents' ability to recall ads, articles, or events they have previously been exposed to.

Reliability: Reliability is the extent to which the measurement process is free from random errors and can be depended on for its accuracy.

Representativeness: The basic sampling criterion specifying that the final sample accurately represents the target population in all significant details.

Respondent characteristics: Data that can be used to describe respondents in terms of demographic, socioeconomic, and psychological characteristics.

Research design: The basic plan which guides the whole research project from planning through data collection to analysis and interpretation.

Research report: The description of the research project and the presentation of the research findings in such a way that it provides information for the decision makers.

Response bias: An inaccurate response caused by a respondent's desire to please the interviewer, or through fatigue or boredom.

Role playing: A technique designed to observe a respondent's behavior when certain conditions exist or information is provided.

Sample: A subgroup of a larger population chosen for the purpose of a survey.

Sampling error: A statistic that measures the difference between the observed probability sample statistic and the population parameter.

Sampling frame: A list of all the sampling units from which the actual sample is drawn.

Sampling unit: The element or elements available for selection at some stage of the sampling process.

Secondary data: Data obtained from published sources, or data which have been collected through other research projects.

Segmentation: Dividing the total sample into subgroups for the purpose of studying variations in responses.

Semantic differential scale: A self-reporting scale requiring the respondent to evaluate an object on a seven-point rating scale bounded on each end by bipolar adjectives.

Sentence completion: A technique in which an incomplete sentence is presented to the respondent who is asked to complete the sentence.

Simple random sampling: A probability sampling procedure where each element has an equal chance of being selected.

Situational factors: Independent variables that are not under the control of the organization, but influence the ministry and results.

Spurious relationship: Relationship that seems to exist between variables, but disappears with detailed analysis.

Standard deviation, s: A measure of dispersion for interval data.

Standard error of the mean: The standard deviation of the sampling distribution of the mean.

Stapel scale: A modification of the semantic differential scale, using a unipolar scale rather than a bipolar scale.

Statistical significance: Differences between two or more responses given by subgroups which are not due to chance.

Straight tabulation: Counting of responses and computation of percentages.

Strata: Subgroups within a population or sample.

Stratified sampling: A two-stage probability sampling procedure in which a heterogeneous population is divided into mutually exclusive and collectively exhaustive strata, and a random sample is drawn from each strata to represent the various groups in the population.

Study population: The aggregate of elements from which the sample is drawn.

Syndicated source: A research organization that provides data to various organizations and companies.

Systematic error: Error that causes a constant bias in the measurements, making the results unreliable.

Table of random numbers: A list of numbers with no internal ordering. Used in selection of a random sample.

Tabulation: Counting of responses and analyzing the responses through various calculations.

Test-retest reliability: Estimating the reliability of a test by repeating the measurement using the same scaling and conditions.

Test units: A group of people involved in an experiment.

Theater tests: Pretesting procedure that exposes respondents to control and test ads in a theater.

Trailer tests: Similar to theater tests, but using a trailer in the vicinity of a shopping mall.

Unaided recall: A questioning approach where the respondent is not provided with any cues to assist recalling the event.

Univariate analysis: The analysis of one variable at a time.

Universe: The target group from which the sample is selected. Another word for population.

Validity: The extent to which the measurement process is free from both systematic and random error and as such valid for the needs of the organization requesting the information.

Variable: A property that takes on different values at different times.

Variance: A measure of the dispersion of the distribution of an interval variable.

Word association: A research technique in which a series of words is presented to the respondent, who is to respond to each one with the first word which comes to mind.

CONCLUSION

All churches and Christian communication organizations need an information system to provide useful data for effective ministry strategy development. We have seen in the preceding chapters that research tools and methodologies are available for gathering such information, and they can be used in church and mission.

Communication research utilizes methodologies and techniques which have primarily been developed by sociological and marketing researchers. Several aspects of anthropological research are also important for certain types of research needed by Christian communicators.

As in other areas of research, we need specific measurement procedures and techniques in order to obtain reliable information. This process is not just an activity carried out by the researcher. The Christian leader must be centrally involved, and the producers should also be involved in the process of media and copy testing. Procedures for such testing are readily available for us to use.

The material in this book has been presented with the hope that the insights provided will both motivate and lead to action so that tools of research can be used to enhance the effectiveness of Christian communication. Our purpose is to see the fulfillment of the commission given by Jesus Christ to communicate the gospel to all people.

SELECTED READINGS

Babbie, Earl. *The Practice of Social Research*. 5th ed. Belmont, California: Wadsworth, 1989.

Engel, James F. *How Can I get Them to Listen*. Grand Rapids: Zondervan, 1977.

Haalund, Ane. *Pretesting Communication Materials*. Rangoon, Burma: UNICEF, 1984.

Kinnear, Thomas C. and Taylor, James F. *Marketing Research, An Applied Approach*. 4th ed. New York: McGraw-Hill, 1991.

Klugh, Henry E. *Statistics: The Essentials for Research*. New York: John Wiley and Sons, 1970.

Pelto, Pertti J. *Anthropological Research, The Structure of Inquiry*. New York: Harper & Row, 1970.

Spradley, James P. *Participant Observation*. New York: Holt, Rinehart and Winston, 1980.

Wimmer, Roger D. and Dominick, Joseph R. *Mass Media Research: An Introduction*. 4th ed. Belmont, California: Wadsworth, 1994.